LOST CIVILIZATIONS

Camelot
EDITORA

GET TO KNOW OUR
BOOKS BY ACCESSING
HERE!

Copyright © 2006 by Manoela Meneses
All rights reserved and protected by law 9.610 of February 2nd,1998.
No part of this book may be reproduced, archived in a search engine, or transmitted by any means, electronic, photocopying, recording or otherwise, without the prior authorization of the rights holder, and it may not be circulated in a form other than that in which it was published, or without the same conditions being imposed on subsequent purchasers.
1st Printing 2022

President: Paulo Roberto Houch
MTB 0083982/SP

Editorial Coordination: Paola Houch and Priscilla Sipans
Translation: Beatriz de Checchi
English text review: Daniel Rabbers
Art Coordination: Rubens Martim (cover)
Edition: Ana Vasconcelos (ECO Editorial)
Layout: Patrícia Andrioli
Images: Shutterstock

The legal deposit has been made.

	International Cataloging in Publication (CIP) data according to ISBD	
C181a	Camelot Editora	
	Lost Civilizations / Camelot Editora. – Barueri : On Line Editora, 2024. 146 p. ; 15,1cm x 23cm.	
	ISBN: 978-65-6095-161-7	
	1. History. I. Title.	
2024-4118		CDD 900 CDU 94
	Elaborated by Vagner Rodolfo da Silva - CRB-8/9410	

Rights reserved to
IBC - Brazilian Institute of Culture LTDA
CNPJ 04.207.648/0001-94
Avenida Juruá 762 – Alphaville Industrial
ZIP: 06455-010 — Barueri/SP
www.editoraonline.com.br

Contents

PRESENTATION 7

VESTIGES FROM THE PAST 9

MACHU PICCHU: SACRED HERITAGE OF THE INCA EMPIRE 23

RAPA NUI'S MILLENAR LEGENDS 31

ARCHITECTURAL HERITAGE OF THE ANASAZIS 41

THE RELIGIOUS VIOLENCE OF MOCHICA SOCIETY 49

THE AKKADIANS' METEORIC RISE 55

TIWANAKU'S AGRICULTURAL EMPIRE 63

VIKING SOCIETY'S CONQUESTS 69

LOST CIVILIZATIONS IN THE AMAZON RAINFOREST 77

CONTROVERSIAL DISCOVERY OF THE CENTURY 85

LIBYA'S ANCIENT HERITAGE 89

THE CULTURAL LEGACY OF MINOAN SOCIETY 95

THE MYSTICAL KINGDOM OF ATLANTIS 103

STORIES AND LEGENDS OF LEMURIA 111

THE CIMMERIAN WARRIORS' BLOODY LEGACY 117

THE MAGICAL UNIVERSE OF SHANGRI-LA 123

THE ISLAND OF MAGIC AND MYSTICISM 129

THE QUEST FOR AGARTTHA'S KINGDOM 135

LESS KNOWN, BUT VERY IMPORTANT 141

LOST WORLDS SHROUDED IN MYSTERIES

The Rapa Nui and their huge moai on Easter Island, the cannibalistic Anasazi in the USA, the Mochica of northern Peru, the nomadic Akkadians, the dreaded Vikings, and legendary places like the lost continent of Atlantis, the myth of Shangri-La, Avalon and "El Dorado", a city filled with gold in the middle of the Amazon jungle. All these civilizations have always inhabited the imagination of researchers and curious people around the world, arousing the interest of historians who try to find out how they came about, how they lived, why they disappeared and even if they really ever existed. What happened, after all, to once-developed people who were buried under layers of mystery?

Many adventurers have risked and lost their lives in search of ruins and treasures of lost civilizations. Some of these cities have been rediscovered and have become tourist hotspots. Others are still part of the world of legends and continue to excite our imagination. In this "Lost Civilizations", you will dive into the past and be surprised by what science has already discovered about these people, of whom today only ruins or even legends remain, but who once forged great civilizations and were the masters of their time.

VESTIGES FROM THE PAST

1

THE SCENARIO OF MYSTERIES INVOLVING VARIOUS ANCIENT CIVILIZATIONS HAS LEFT TRAILS OF LEGENDS AND FANTASTIC STORIES TO BE UNRAVELLED AROUND THE WORLD

The way of life adopted by contemporary society is directly linked to the activities carried out by civilizations lost in the past. Forward-thinking, each of them had to adapt to a series of natural events to generate an efficient system of functioning. Over the centuries, archaeological studies have revealed historical legacies left by ancient cities throughout the trajectory of humanity, many of which remain evident to this day. From the very beginning, the hierarchical scenario of its inhabitants was already represented by strong divisions of power between government elites and simple men focused on manual services, acting at different scales of planting activities.

The customs of primitive populations involved peculiar cultures revealed in very different ways. Many developed their own languages, specialised centres in commercial movements, involving the main exchange currencies of each era. The development process provided inventions considered modern in the face of the limited resources available in primitive cities. With no structure to face disasters caused by climatic factors, people innovated by creating drought methods, irrigation techniques, clay protection against floods and the maintenance of river channels that ensured the preservation of water in times of prolonged drought. The feeding routine of individuals also presented the need to produce domestic utensils such as ceramic pots to store and process meals.

Although the advances made have been successful, entire civilizations have disappeared, in some cases without leaving any trace of their existence. Natural disasters, widespread famine, violent invasions, wars, decline of resources extracted from the environment, overpopulation and epidemics represent some of the main causes of extinction. The evidence left by past habits revolves around various legends and mysteries fuelled by archaeological discoveries surrounding the rise, heyday and decline of ancient societies. In some situations, new evidence even alters already known historical records.

MATHEMATICAL BEGINNINGS

From 3800 BC, the Sumerians began building what historians believe to be the first civilization of the ancient world. Established in Lower Mesopotamia, a region located on the border between the Tigris and Euphrates rivers, the native peoples built a developed social and cultural system around important cities such as Nippur, Kish, Uruk and Ur. The inhabitants of the region now the territory of Iraq, were responsible for numerous creative solutions to improve the quality of life without any technological resources available at the time. Among the innovative services were homemade ovens, wheeled vehicles and even watercraft. The first written records, made on clay tablets hardened by the sun, are also elements in

Sumer's success story. In trade, valuable metals were brought from other places and sold in barter schemes with interest payments, even though there was no currency.

It was during this time of expansion that early traders developed mathematical solutions that are used in different sectors of contemporary life. Administrative advances allowed the region's traders to participate in the development of square roots, fractions with the number 1, the Pythagorean table and the sexagesimal system, which originated from various exact techniques. In addition to financial transactions, all this knowledge was used to help control river waters, preventing flooding during the flood season by creating river channels. Barrier methods facilitated navigation by increasing the entry of products used to supply the population. Another legacy left by the Sumerians is the format of the hour divided into 60 minutes and the 360-degree angle.

INTERNAL WARS

With the rapid growth of the region's population, Sumer expanded into the surrounding territories, forming several cities. Great kingdoms were built, resulting in violent governmental confrontations. The recurrence of bloody wars led by the inhabitants of Lagash and Ur made it possible for Semitic people to enter in the territory. Around 2350 BC, Akkadian representatives dominated Sumer, constituting the rise of the Akkadian Empire, the first great state of the Mesopotamia.

ACCORDING TO THE BIBLE

Approached in the gospel stories as the world's first civilization, ancient Egypt stood out by forming a strong state system. According to the chapters of the Holy Book, its inhabitants laid all the founda-

---

In addition to their scientific, literary, and social contributions, the Sumerians were also responsible for the invention of beer. Canadian archaeologists discovered this through a chemical examination of a residual layer of pottery found in western Iran. The study was led by the University of Pennsylvania and concluded that the object served as a container for storing the drink between 3500 and 3100 BC.

tions for the rise of Israel. The prophet Moses, responsible for writing the first five texts of the Bible, was born, and educated, among Egyptian society. Completely adept at agriculture, the population depended minimally on practices such as fishing and hunting to sustain themselves, and were considered pioneers in domesticating wild species of animals. Located in the northeast of Africa, the population's progress was also due to the water resources offered by the river Nile. The system of menial labour made it possible to increase the land conquered by peasants who cultivated grapes, papyrus, wheat, barley, and vegetables.

The presence of a centralized state in power, through the leadership of the pharaoh, forced farmers to set aside part of their produce for the government. Between 5000 and 3000 BC there were already large numbers of people living around fortified buildings and temples. The desert climate protected them from foreign invasions and the river floods did not destructively affect the region, serving as a thermometer for the irrigation system of the crops.

From a commercial point of view, they hardly depended on foreign relations. The fertilized soil had a vast supply of copper, gold, and other minerals. The entire population of the time revolved around the emblematic figure of the pharaoh. The monarch promoted himself as a true heir to divine will, acting in military, judicial, religious, and political areas. In 2150 BC, several factors led to the process that culminated in the complete decay of the Egyptian monarchy. The country was temporarily divided after Asian invasions, resulting in the disappearance of the social customs established by the ancient civilization.

HISTORICAL MONUMENTS

One of the most popular lost civilizations among today's travellers is the territory of Machu Picchu. Also known as the lost city of the Incas, it is located on top of a mountain at an altitude of 7,872 feet in Peru. Since 2007, the monument has been on the list of the seven wonders of the modern world, symbolizing the cultural value of its past and its many contributions to the evolution of the archaeological scenario. The entire historic region was built with stones gathered by the Inca Empire in the 15th century. The harsh religious system imposed at the time inspired the construction of houses, churches, squares, and cemeteries. Each location was strategically placed to connect the inhabitants with the divine will in worship of the Sun god.

In addition to the religious areas, the Incas also invested in the maintenance of large terraces used for farming. For those who visit

Egyptian scriptures produced at the dawn of their civilization

Machu Picchu, considered one of the most important tourist attractions in Latin America, it is possible to see only 30% of its original architecture, divided between agricultural areas and commercial centres, which are currently in ruins. There are various theories about the disappearance of the city, but it is believed that most of its legacy was lost or modified by the Spanish and the native governments of the region.

MYSTERIOUS ISOLATION

The trajectory of the people of Easter Island, in the Pacific Ocean, shows the fury of nature against the inappropriate advances of humanity. Rising between the 11th and 14th centuries, the society baptized as Rapa Nui became known for being one of the most remote points in the world. Belonging to Chile, the complex territory covers 1,786.8 square feet and is located 2,294 miles from the American continent. As if its geographical isolation was not enough, the island is also surrounded by several natural events that prevent the soil from being fertile and make it impossible to grow food.

According to a succession of theories, the process of occupation of Rapa Nui took place between the 5th and 8th centuries. The case of greatest curiosity about the characteristics presented by the natives is involved with the construction of the Moai statues. Many legends portray the stratospherically large sculptures as the faces of deceased people belonging to ruling dynasties in the monarchical system in force. Numerous factors contributed to the decay of the Pashto civilization, the most widely accepted being the people's lack of care for the preservation of the forests and the exacerbated growth of the number of inhabitants.

CANNIBALISTIC PRACTICES

Developed in the southwest of the United States, today occupied by the states of Colorado, New Mexico, Arizona and Utah, Anasazi society began its activities from the year 100 BC. The indigenous people were apparently unaware of all forms of writing, the uses of the wheel and the progress made in the field of metallurgy. The structure of the civilization's survival consisted of weaving cotton, generating intense trade with other nearby towns. Over the years they also became known for their ingenious cliff-top buildings, pottery, and carpet-making.

In September 2000, an excavation program carried out in an ancient village in Colorado uncovered acts of anthropophagy among the Indians. Around the year 1150, the American village was in decline and was abandoned by most of its inhabitants. The results of anthropological studies indicate that, at that time, seven people were killed, cooked, and served as food in Anasazi meals. The evidence represents the first cannibalistic activities among the primitive civilizations of the United States.

WILD NATURE

The Mochica were so influential that their achievements are still acclaimed today. Residing in northern Peru, they established a solid model of an active state between the 1st and 7th centuries. The construction of the empire was entirely centred on the verdicts defined by the nobility. A surprising combination of ideals transformed the population into exemplary agricultural producers. The land was cultivated thanks to the creation of aqueducts, responsible for bringing water from fountains to public and private places. Among the foods they planted abundantly were beans, corn, and potatoes. The Mochica were pioneers in the development of clay pots, propagating reproduction techniques with human traits. To this day, groups of historians are looking for exact explanations of the events that led to their disappearance. One of the most accepted theories is that the Mochica were attacked by nature during long periods of drought and flood.

Details found in ruins in the Mochica region of Peru

UNIFICATION OF THE EMPIRE

Around 2250 BC, the Mesopotamian region was the scene of a serious conflict. With the arrival of the nomadic tribe of Akkadians, the Sumerians were forced to engage in an extensive period of warfare in order not to lose control of the fertile lands there. Researchers suggest that the invaders migrated from northern Syria in search of valuable natural resources to build a potential empire. Faced with the disunity displayed by the Sumerian leaders, the Akkadian victory was soon formalized. Although initially adversaries, the similar culture between the two groups made it possible to unify all the inhabitants, forming the first Mesopotamian empire.

Under the rule of King Sargon I, this period became known as the Sumero-Akkadian civilization. Beliefs and arts contemplated the gods and animals through the construction of palaces integrated with important temples. Economic progress consisted of successful agricultural solutions interspersed with cultural activities carried out in cuneiform writing. The whole structure of society went into decline after a series of internal revolts caused by discontent among the people. The Akkadian empire did not survive violent foreign invasions and disappeared two centuries after its first steps.

WORLD HERITAGE

Impressive ruins now occupy the territorial space left by one of South America's most enduring civilizations. The people of Tiwanaku thrived around Lake Titicaca, on the border between present-day Peru and Bolivia, building an important kingdom. During its period of ascendancy in the 500s and 900s, the city stands out archaeologically for its historic public structure for contemporary concepts. The ancient region had elements of an expressive conglomerate, initially home between 30 to 40 thousand inhabitants.

One of its main architectural creations, the Akapana pyramid is associated with long periods of drought alternating with heavy flooding. Around the famous monument there are numerous drainage facilitation schemes formed by dykes specialized in draining the water coming from the river channels. Extinct after a severe climate crisis, the city of Tiwanaku was classified as a UNESCO World Heritage Site. Dissatisfied with the deteriorated state of the legendary ruins, the organization proposed a restoration program for the region, which began in 2009.

MULTIPLE TALENTS

Figures in popular imagination, the inhabitants of Nordic Greenland became known for their various activities. Coming from Europe, the immigrants created a model of life extremely similar to that of their homeland. The civilization was formed by the Vikings, very conservative warriors who were famous for their violence in solving everyday problems. The first contacts between the Vikings and the natives of the area are reminiscent of intense conflicts and bloodbaths. The political scenario divided sovereignty between the clergy and influential leaders of the ancient city.

Tiwanaku ruins in the Bolivia-Chile border region

Rocks with ancient drawings in Utah, United States

Trade rules functioned without any kind of currency, in the form of simple exchanges of products between local farms. At the height of the Viking period, there were around 250 properties with 20 people living at each one. The return of the traditional cold climate directly affected the increase in resources taken from the environment. Gradually, the island became more and more isolated as it suffered from the harsh winter. The Vikings' difficulty in adapting to the cultural evolution that was perpetuating throughout the world also helped to bring about the community's extinction. Almost all of them died, but for archaeologists, the peculiar behaviour they adopted continues to gather many legends and mysteries.

BRAZILIAN PAST

Before it was discovered by Europeans in the 16th century, the Amazon was home to more than 7 million people. Geological researchers claim that the indigenous tribes of the time practiced advanced activities, given the scarcity of materials available in the forest. Traders working on a large scale projects, the most famous communities were the Marajoara, from the island of Marajó, and the Tapajônica communities, located where the city of Santarém is today. The production of ceramics was the main indigenous activity in the region and was distributed to various parts of the world. The progress made by the village led to the growth of a wealthy empire that began its civilization more than 1000 years before the first Portuguese arrived in Brazil.

Through the remains found by archaeology, it is possible to identify a careful artistic eye transformed into objects made of clay that reveal their customs. With a larger population, the Tapajós acted as sovereigns in the Amazonian "El Dorado." The population was so large that the Tapajós leaders could gather around 60,000 men willing to take part in battles. The Marajoaras' talents were focused on engineering achievements. Their interests went beyond building the village's existing huts, and they also worked on improving the island against flooding by making structural embankments on the land. Despite the evolutionary process, they were unable to resist the arrival of the Portuguese colonizers and became extinct, leaving behind a multitude of stories that have an impact on today's society.

ENIGMATIC RESEARCHES

Surrounded by mysteries, possible traces of an ancient civilization located in the Honduran jungle were discovered in 2012 by archaeological excavations. The structure of the city of the Monkey God, also known as The White City, may have been covered up to this day, making it impossible to see the houses, leafy trees, stones, palaces, and various sculptures with important cultural significance. The first pieces revealed in 2016 prove the existence of human life in the area thanks to the head of a jaguar and a vessel adorned around pieces of birds. The site studied by science was hidden in the virgin lands of the Honduran jungle. The Honduran government has enlisted the help of experts from National Geographic and the American University of Colorado in the project to reveal ancient ways of human coexistence. It is speculated that the civilization existed between 3000 BC and 900 AD. The legend of the White City's population even appears in Honduran students' textbooks, referred to as the Central American Amazon.

LOST EMPIRE

After a long period of armed conflict, British archaeological groups were able to resume their research in southwest Libya in 2011. In search of signs that prove the past of more than 100 influential civilizations in the desert, the activities used images captured by aircraft and modern satellite systems. The project is funded by the European Union, with available resources estimated at US$4 million. The first finds are in the city of Germa, identified in the past by the name of Garaman. Established around the 6th century BC, the Garaman settlement has gone down in history as a civilization formed by barbaric and sedentary men. However, the remains of these other cities show an extremely enterprising version of the region, working hard to create a network of sophisticated cities. Many ruins became known to archaeology more than 30 years ago, but researchers were only able to study their influence on the country's culture after the end of the wars led by Muammar Gaddafi's government. Among the remains left by the former inhabitants, the most impressive are the castles up to four meters high, cemeteries and plantation marks.

GREEK BEGINNINGS

Europe's first naval power, the Minoan civilization existed between 2700 and 1450 BC. Considered the main representatives of Greek culture, they evolved socially on the island of Crete, choosing Knossos as their main city. Literate in various forms of writing that have never been deciphered by researchers, they sold high-end goods to regions in Egypt and the Near East. In addition to their successful marketing system, they also worked on solutions for water transportation and the construction of large palaces, considered architecturally advanced given the resources available at the time.

To this day, little is known about the origin of the Minoan population. Living for the most part on the Aegean Island, they reached their peak around 1700 BC, when an earthquake reached as far as the area, devastating the palaces and the entire structure of cattle, goat, and agricultural farming. They soon rebuilt everything with even more benefits. The decline of civilization came at the end of the Neopalatial period, during a cultural crisis that allowed all the palaces to be demolished. Natural forces, such as the explosion of a volcano, later contributed to the total disappearance of the people.

MYSTERIOUS TALES

Even centuries after it was first mentioned by Plato, the lost city of Atlantis continues to arouse interest in the contemporary scientific world. The legendary metropolis is said to have been wiped out by a devastating tsunami that wiped out more than 62 miles of territory. To find the exact location of the remains, the researchers analysed photos taken by satellites that revealed the best search points north of Cádiz, Spain. Maps buried in the wilderness of Doña Ana Park may have shown the practices of the civilization. All the discoveries show several cities built as a kind of memorial to customs related to the ancient inhabitants.

The survivors of the natural tragedy would have built new urbanizations inside the area. Various theories point to the lost city as the first man--made metropolis. Little is known about the way of life of the inhabitants of Atlantis; however, Plato's tales describe the settlement as a naval power powerful enough to conquer many parts of western Europe and Africa in approximately 9600 BC. Some legends claim that the Greek philosopher used true stories in the development of his works, such as the eruption of Thera and the Trojan War.

AQUATIC IMMENSITY

According to archaeologist Augustus Le Plongeon, the continent of Mu, also known as Lemuria, is responsible for the origin of all human beings. The series of legends disseminated in 1896 on the subject conflict with the version of the researchers, who claim to be unaware of this civilization, which became extinct in the early days of the American continent. However, some scholars are still looking for evidence of the geological changes responsible for sinking Mu's territory into the ocean. The city's inhabitants would have formed an extremely developed society around 50,000 years ago, having become rich trading gold, silver, and copper. With evolved knowledge, the leaders of the population would have foreseen the catastrophe by coordinating a large escape group to travel aimlessly around the world. The sovereign goddess among all the gods in Egyptian mythology, Mut, was one of the founding immigrants of Central America and, later, of several countries. The most famous legend is that Mut was a remnant of the Garden of Eden, described in the Bible as a space created by God to house Adam and Eve.

INTERNAL DISPUTES

Another indigenous community that was the protagonist of great internal wars were the Cimmerians. Their origins have yet to be confirmed by archaeology, and they lived north of the Caucasus, the name given to a region located between the Black Sea and the Caspian Sea, marking the borders of Europe and Asia. The history of the society began in 1300 BC in an area taken up by the Pontic steppes, formed by vegetated plains. Expelled from their lands by the Scythians, a people made up of nomads from classical antiquity, they migrated south. From this episode onwards, they remained on pilgrimage for a long time, attacking potential territories. Several disputes between groups of Cimmerian chieftains over the leadership of the tribe caused the rapid decline of civilization.

MYSTICISM IN THE HIMALAYAS

A series of legends surround the elements that make up the story of the village known as Shangri-la. Created by the imagination of writer James Hilton, the literary work deals with a magical point in the universe supposedly located in the Himalayan Mountain ranges. Faced with a paradisiacal and completely peaceful setting considered unattainable for human beings, time runs differently, making it impossible for all the inhabitants to age as in the rest of the world. The myth arose shortly after the release of the book "Lost Horizon" in 1925. Inspired by the descriptions in the book, countless tourists organized expeditions to try and find this enigmatic paradise. The civilization is said to live around a place in Tibet known as Digging, which was possibly used as the basis for the literary composition of the mystical refuge. Given the many similarities between fiction and reality, in 2001 the city was officially renamed Shangri-la.

LITERARY TRAIL

The legendary island of Avalon is a source of popular curiosity because of the mysterious references to its stunning apples. In the world-famous literary story of King Arthur, the place is mentioned for the first time in Geoffrey of Monmouth's "Historia Regum Britanniae" of 1508. Described as a region of brave men and adventurers, it has also been associated with immortal beings in various theories. The Tor Hill in Glastonbury, England, was considered by history buffs to be one of the access points to the expanse of Avalon. It is speculated that the ocean surrounded all parts of the region, serving as a spiritual resting place for the dead before being reborn in the flesh. Another way to reach the enchanted village is by entering a cave in the side of a mountain. Mixing real elements and imaginary scripts, Avalon continues to arouse the interest among fans of places full of magic.

LEGENDARY CITY

Theories about the famous kingdom of Agarttha claim that the territory is hidden inside the Earth. For some scholars, the planet's surface is formed by a complex system of tunnels and caves located in the Himalayan region. Despite being considered a myth in Eastern culture, the civilization was first mentioned by French writer Louis Jacolliot. In 1873, he created the legend of a mysterious city in India that would only exist in hidden places. Initially, the village functioned as a kind of mystical residence occupied by Norse gods.

The story became popular through the book "Beasts, Men and Gods" by Polish science teacher Ferdynand Ossendowski. The kingdom, which supposedly mixes fictional and real events, is home to millions of beings under the command of the King of the World. In addition to Eastern countries, several occultists defend the veracity of the story of Agarttha, which has been disseminated in renowned literary productions. The only means of access would be a secret portal, exterminating all possibilities for evil to enter. The inhabitants can develop powers to control the Earth, thus preventing the population from discovering their presence.

LOST CIVILIZATIONS

MACHU PICCHU: SACRED HERITAGE OF THE INCA EMPIRE

2

MYTHS AND LANDSCAPES, THE LOST CITY OF MACHU PICCHU ENCHANTS THOUSANDS OF TOURISTS AS ONE OF THE SEVEN WONDERS OF THE MODERN WORLD

The mysterious trails of Machu Picchu represent a large part of the cultural history of the Inca Empire. Discovered in 1911 by the American anthropologist Hiram Bingham, this ancient civilization was at its peak before the first Europeans arrived in America. The meticulous architecture of the rock-faced constructions attracts tourists from all over the world, looking to appreciate monuments of extreme historical richness.

During the supremacy of the Inca population, the city was strategically erected 69.44 miles from the capital, Cusco, which functioned as the main commercial and political seat of government at the time. Many theories surround Machu Picchu's role in society. Some speculate that the site served only as a centre for astronomical studies and venues for religious services. Researchers, on the other hand, report the city's role as an important metropolis that housed several powerful names sent by the monarchs for an administrative centre hierarchy. Due to its completely isolated position at the top of the Andes, at an altitude of 7,874.4 feet, the community escaped unscathed from the violent actions of colonizers.

ARCHAEOLOGICAL STUDIES

Soon after finding the traces left by the inhabitants of the past, anthropologist Hiram Bingham managed to collect around 500 ceramic pots and

The traditional llamas in Machu Picchu territory

The lost city of Machu Picchu, one of the seven wonders of the modern world

200 models of other objects used by the inhabitants of the village. Every piece of evidence proves the Incas' connection to a system of protection for the most influential figures of the ruling nobility, preserved by the belief in proximity to the divinities established by nature. The view from the top of the mountain shows how Machu Picchu functioned in its days as an isolated metropolis. It is even speculated that the choice to create a city on such an elevated structure was strategically designed to bring humans closer to heaven. It is not known exactly when Machu Picchu's activities began, but geological research indicates that around 1000 BC there was already a community operating in the region now occupied by Cusco. The territory controlled by the empire's lost metropolis stretched from the north of Ecuador to central Chile.

INCA BUILDINGS

Military meetings convened with the aim of conquering other communities were held in the city, from where all the troops at the time left. After the arrival of the Spanish colonizers in 1532, the Inca Empire was going through a strong political crisis, aggravated by the presence of invaders in most of its provinces. Even with the frequent episodes of disagreement, the Europeans only managed to take power of the Empire four decades later, without ever finding Machu Picchu. Even today, you can see in the ruin's details chosen by the Incas in the construction of the city's monuments. Inside many of the houses, the architecture indicates walls made of stone structures fitted together very precisely, without the aid of any type of mortar.

One of the most visited spots by tourists is the rock of Intihuatana, famous for serving as a method of locating society in time. Annual sacred events and astronomical rituals were celebrated there. Legends also claim that the stone's mystical power attracted many animal and human sacrifices. Another monument is the Temple of the Three Windows and the Priest's House. Every detail of the workmanship of the environment is impressive with the care taken to build the structures. The Inca Palace hosted the great leaders of the empire when they visited the monarchs. Overlooking the eastern part of Machu Picchu, the site has vestiges similar to those of luxurious hotels, housing reserved rooms, dining areas, bathrooms and an area dedicated to servants.

SOCIAL ACTIVITIES

Machu Picchu's territory is divided between rural areas located to the east and urbanized extensions. Each building was limited by walls at maximum 1,312.4 feet long. During the active period of civilization, its inhabitants lived mainly from resources derived from agricultural

Ruins of the lost city

Monuments constructed by stone in Machu Picchu

activities.One of the most common jobs in the city was planting corn. As there were no flat areas on the way up the mountain, farmers had to build makeshift areas on the slopes. In all the fields, the only water used for irrigation came from the rain. The animals used for daily chores, such as the llama and alpaca, were domesticated before being used as merchandise.

RELIGIOUS SPACE

Many legends portray Machu Picchu as only a place prepared by the Incas for religious services. The main entrance to the city was represented by the expansion of the Sun Gate. The point separated the commercial and agricultural areas. Extremely faithful to their beliefs, the population used animals to celebrate fertility and some of their temples symbolized the land of the living and the dead. The space for the deities was separate to represent the supremacy of the Sun god, the most popular among the Incas at the time. Various monuments sculpted in gold were used to bring the sun's luminosity into the metropolis as a form of religious respect. The Temple of the Sun had two strategically placed windows, marking ceremonies during the arrival of the first rays of summer and winter.

ELITIST DIVISION

The noble area of the metropolis was home to the emperor's family, official soldiers and priests invited by the nobility. The rapid increase in population made it difficult to produce food for all areas of the city. Troops of llamas brought food from neighbouring communities to supply the wealthy residents. The humblest people built their homes in the lower part of Machu Picchu. One of the great secrets to resisting the side effects of the altitude was the planting of coca leaves, which are still offered to tourists during the pilgrimage. The harsh climate is hard on visitors, who are constantly approached by locals selling food and water along the way. Quechua, the language of the Incas, is still spoken by many of Cusco's residents, and many of them use it to show travellers details of their culture, charging for the service.

CREATIVE ENGINEERING

In order to build the monuments only with stones fitted together without any type of foundation, the inhabitants of Machu Picchu used rocks found in the mountain's soil, which is rich in different types of granite. The techniques used by the Incas to extract the material from the ground involved filling natural fissures with water, waiting for the liquid to freeze in the face of the low night-time temperatures and facilitating the process of extracting the rocks. Little is known about how the materials were transported around the city. At the time of its demise, the civilization had around 1,200 inhabitants, a figure considered low compared to the large population of the Inca Empire, which numbered 12 million people. Although there are many theories about the decline of Machu Picchu's population, the one most accepted by archaeologists says that the city was taken over by a serious smallpox epidemic. Today, the sacred site operates under special care by the Peruvian government.

Inca Trail to Machu Picchu

FROM BRAZIL TO MACHU PICCHU

The logistics are not the easiest, but all tourists guarantee that the trip to one of the seven wonders of the world is worth every moment. Get to know the route:

Leaving Brazil, travellers need to take a plane to Lima, the capital of Peru. Capitals such as Rio de Janeiro, São Paulo and Porto Alegre offer non-stop flights to Lima, which take approximately five hours. When you arrive in Lima, you need to take another plane to Cusco International Airport. The journey takes approximately one hour. Another option is to fly to Bolivia and take the traditional Death Train to Peru. This route has become very popular among backpackers with less money for the trip. If you choose to complete the route by bus, it can take more than 24 hours on the road to reach Cusco.

Once in the city of Cusco, transportation to Aguas Calientes, the village closest to the ruins of Machu Picchu, can be done by bus or train, covering 59.52 miles. Both options offer large windows so that tourists can enjoy the view of historic landmarks along the way.

The journey from Aguas Calientes to Machu Picchu is made by minibus. The journey takes about 20 minutes to the park that houses the archaeological site with the ruins. For the more adventurous, the best way is to take the Inca trail, walking for four days following various monuments built by the civilization.

Despite the symptoms caused by the altitude, such as diarrhea, nausea and dizziness, the view and the historical content make the 26.04 miles rewarding once you reach the top of the mountain. At the end of the climb, it takes about an hour to see the extent of the ruins of the lost city.

RAPA NUI'S MILLENAR LEGENDS

3

IN ONE OF THE MOST ISOLATED SPOTS ON THE PLANET, THE SOCIETY FORMED ON EASTER ISLAND DEVELOPED ITS OWN RELIGIOUS CONCEPTS RESULTING IN A MAJOR ENVIRONMENTAL IMPACT CRISIS

Every piece of history on Easter Island reveals peculiar details about all the phases experienced by the Rapa Nui people. The ancient civilization emerged in one of the most isolated territories on the planet based on countless creative events to facilitate its independent system of survival. Called the "navel of the world" by the native inhabitants, the lost city occupies a very small space in the Pacific Ocean, located on the path between South America and Polynesia. Although it belongs to the Chilean map, the island's cultural growth is directly linked to the customs developed by the Polynesians. The process of apogee and decline of the Rapa Nui community represents for today's society the extreme importance of preserving the resources extracted from natural sources. After several studies carried out by ethnographers, it was concluded that the first people on the island landed on Anakena beach after a long sea voyage in double-hulled boats at the beginning of the 5th century. It is also speculated that the animals used in the trade and food system of the Easter Island inhabitants were brought to the site by Polynesian tribes passing through the region.

SPIRITUAL ORIGINS

The civilization's trajectory impresses with its connection to religious elements. Anthropologists suggest that the iconic Moai statues were initially built to venerate their ancestors. The immense wooden sculptures had features similar to human faces and symbolized the belief and power of the dynasties made up of the inhabitants of the place. The handiwork was carried out near the craters of a volcano and transported to altars built by the sea to celebrate the religious activities of each village. Little is known about the solutions the villagers found to lower their giant works to the desired location. Each image represented a deceased member of the families in various parts of the island, creating a kind of competition as to who could develop the most artistically complex sculpture.

Some archaeologists believe that the Moai were laid on their backs and pushed over rocks along a path that could stretch for days over distances of up to 12.4 miles. The chosen method of movement severely damaged all the trees and rocks on the ground, as the gigantic sculptures bumped into various parts of the environment while moving. Some of them weighed as much as 595,350 pounds and were 29.53 feet tall. The main precepts of these people are still preserved today in the remaining expanses of Easter Island. Open to tourists, the region is still impressive visually with its natural beauty and the immensity of its sculptures, which have stood the test of time.

Features drawn in the sculptures by the inhabitants of Rapa Nui

CULTURAL IMPASSE

During the heyday of the Rapa Nui civilization, the inhabitants of other Polynesian islands fought over the domains of each territory, divided amongst 12 communities. The losing dynasty had to make its way to the next uninhabited island in precarious boats with few resources. It is believed that the first people arrived on Easter Island around the year 900. Native stories passed down orally by locals say that the pioneers landed in an expedition led by the figure of Hotu Matu'a, considered the great father of this ancient civilization. In one or two canoes, the settler travelled with his wife, six children and a few other relatives. All they brought from their homeland were pieces of sugar cane, chickens, and rats that invaded the boat. Legend has it that he lived on as a great king of the village, only to be replaced after his death by his descendants. The Moai made in honour of the members of this dynasty face the sea, as if they are still looking out over the island from some other spiritual plane.

FUNCTIONAL SYSTEM

In recent research into the vegetation of Easter Island, groups of archaeologists have discovered that the territory had a large green area during the active period of the Rapa Nui civilization. It was even home to the largest species of palm tree in the world. The climate was mild most of the time, but cold by Polynesian standards. In addition to the volcanic lava and the beach, the city also had a tropical forest with more than 21 types of trees. The population lived in houses built from wood, dried le-

Moai in the Rano Raraku region, Easter Island

aves, and straw. In its heyday, Rapa Nui society supplied itself with food grown on its own land.

GREAT FEASTS

One of the foods most consumed by the inhabitants was sweet potatoes. The villages with the most resources accumulated large chicken farms. At the time, the animal was seen as an important bargaining chip and was housed in areas surrounded by rocks. It is estimated that the community had more than 15,000 people producing food in abundance. As well as being physically demanding, working on the stones also required extensive ropes made from tree bark to place the monuments. In the summer, dolphins and fish appeared on the coast, guaranteeing great feasts for the inhabitants of Rapa Nui. The period in which there was an increase in natural foods consumed by the natives coincided with the peak of Moai production, between 1400 and 1600.

ENVIRONMENTAL DIFFICULTIES

Over time, unbridled population growth became a problem for the island's routine. The constant environmental aggression practiced against the trees during the construction of the Moai statues reduced the number of birds and, consequently, the flowering of new plants in the region's forest. The feeding system presented serious difficulties, accentuated by the isolated geographical structure of the site. The mild climate most of the time gave way to a long winter season. The icy waters of the ocean made it difficult to find fish in the region. Without resources, the population also suffered from the strong winds around the rocky slopes. This difficult time resulted in the death of most of the trees in the forest. Faced with a shortage of wood and stone, the locals were no longer able to produce fishing rods made from the leftover material used in the moai. The size of Easter Island became too small to comfortably house all its inhabitants and several areas of green forest had to be destroyed to open new living spaces. Without specific knowledge of how destroyed vegetation regenerates, they believed that it would all come back in a short time.

COLLAPSE ANNOUNCED

The extinction of the island's main raw material had an impact on the creation of canoes, built from wood and used for fishing in more remote locations. Other foods consumed daily by the inhabitants were poultry and seal meat. To cook their meals, they burned wood from the forest. The glorious palm trees were also uprooted, severely damaging the soil, and leaving the land exposed to the sun. As the fertile areas declined, many villages began to starve, as nothing around them grew agricultural crops. The end of Easter Island's ecosystem generated a climate of tension among the population, starting a succession of internal wars. From then on, cannibalistic methods entered the routine of the Rapa Nui civilization.

Without anything to eat, the enemies killed in the conflict became the meal of the victorious village. The final act consisted of tearing down the Moai statues of the opponent, considered the greatest symbol of humiliation in the village. Even without any social structure, the island continued to receive expeditions during its period of decadence. Pests brought by European visitors contributed to the death of many natives who were not immunologically prepared to deal with modern diseases. Every available natural resource was fought over by the surviving dynasties in bloody fashion. Hungry, they harassed travellers who landed there. In 1862, Peruvian slave traders kidnapped half the population, further exacerbating the crisis.

According to records published by missionaries, by 1877 only 111 people lived in the Easter Island region. Power was seized by a kind of militia, the Matatoa, who adopted the belief in a different god from the natives. Stones that had been considered sacred until then were now used to prevent gusts of wind from hitting crops. As a total sign of disrespect, the invaders drew female body features and symbols in homage to male birds on the remaining Moai sculptures. The aggressive attitude was a way of replacing the figures of ancestors with the new deities. Survivors of some villages had to go and live in caves in order to

> One of the most important customs of the Rapa Nui civilization was the peculiar choice of the community's sovereign leader. 0.992 miles away from Easter Island, representatives of the village's most influential families competed in a competition in the region's sea. The competitor who managed to swim the entire course and bring a swallow's egg back to the starting point intact won.

escape the chaos prevailing in the community. The huge stone images gave way to small artistic sculptures, the Kavakava Moai, created as a reflection of the population of that period, with obvious ribs and thin faces.

MOAI LEGENDS

Many speculations surround the trajectory of Rapa Nui over the centuries. Some researchers believe that the population knew very well what they were doing when they cut down a large part of the forest to build new houses. According to theories, the inhabitants of the civilization were actually very talented agricultural engineers. The natural fields were often fertilized with substances extracted from volcanic larvae. Although Easter Islanders destroyed green areas in the process of urbanization, they took care to fit pastures into the expanse. In a study carried out by anthropologist Mara Mulrooney, a series of pieces of evidence point to the decay of the settlement only after the definitive arrival of the European colonizers, overturning the idea that the entire structure collapsed in the face of nature's fury.

One of Easter Island's volcanic areas

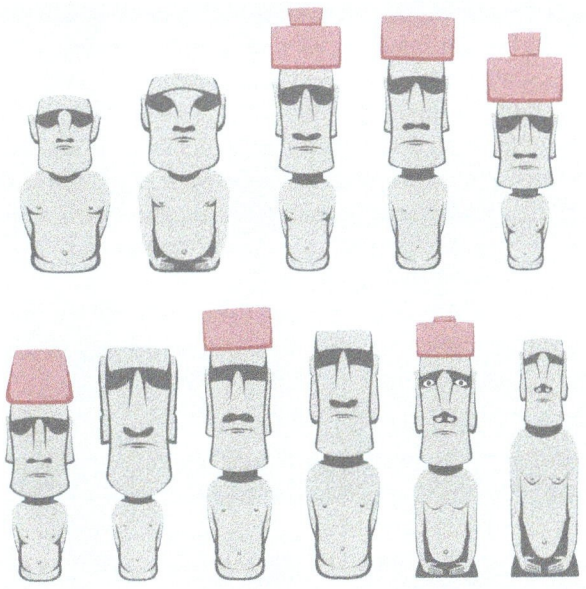
Various forms of Moai statues built over time

COLONIZING EXPEDITIONS

The name Easter Island was given by Dutch navigator Jacob Roggeveen. On seeing the civilization on the paradisiacal beach on an Easter Sunday in 1722, he was impressed by all the elements that made up the scenery, especially the immense Moai statues. Immersed by the artistic creativity of the local inhabitants, he decided to name it after the commemorative date. At the time, the explorer reported that around 2,500 natives greeted his crew with calm and kind greetings, even though they lived in a very humble situation. For more than 150 years after it was discovered, at least 53 other expeditions from various corners of Europe passed through Easter Island. When the Dutch arrived on Easter Island, the civilization began a second phase of complete decline caused by natural disasters, wars, diseases, and kidnappings. All oral culture and the beginnings of writing were lost from 1864 onwards, after the missionaries began their activities with the Easter Island children.

VARIOUS THEORIES

Over the centuries, Easter Island has become one of the favourite places for archaeologists in search of historical evidence. Among many legends, the remains left by this civilization have also become part of the popular imagination. One of the best-known theories about the Rapa Nui involves extraterrestrials. The Moai sculptures are said to have been inspired by the figure of beings from other planets in their artistic conception. For the writer Erich von Daniken, primitive societies could not have built so many things without any effective reference to work centred on strength and intelligence. However, all the research carried out on the island indicates that the stones used to build the monuments were taken from the local soil, from an extinct volcano. Some myths also refer to the influence of rats in the process of the territory's decline. During the period of their rise, Easter Island had an abundance of food and practically no predators. The situation was considered ideal for the mass proliferation of rats, which emerged from the groups that landed with the island's first inhabitants. With no natural predators, the animals were responsible for preventing the trees from sprouting again by eating the new plants as soon as they appeared on the ground.

ALTERNATIVE PROBLEMS

The failure of the ecosystem on Easter Island is currently being held up as an example of the excesses committed in today's world. Many scholars differ on the reasons that triggered its decline, but none of them fail to point out the danger of using natural resources without a great deal of planning to avoid imbalances. The most widely accepted version of the final events on Rapa Nui preaches a combination of several degrading situations. In addition to the lack of knowledge about natural resources, the island's population was also exploited by its colonizers and succumbed to the disappearance of most of its inhabitants.

Moai statues from the back

REPLICAS OF THE PAST

In the mid-1980s, groups of researchers began an intensive program into the ways in which the Moai were built and transported around Easter Island. Initially, they developed statues similar to the originals, with practically the same height and weight dimensions, and tried to push them through the rocks using tools available in the past.

During the experiment, given the difficulty of transportation, they concluded that it was impossible for the oai to have been moved to the ceremonial areas by rolling down the rocks. In 1987, American archaeologist Charles Love managed to move a 20,000-pound statue using an improvised vehicle accompanied by two sleds similar to those that may have existed during the height of civilization. Supported by huge ropes, he and 25 other men managed to drag the replica by hand for just 150.926 over two minutes.

Ten years later, Norwegian adventurer Thor Heyerdahl, accompanied by Czech engineer Pavel Pavel, built another replica to try to reassemble the of the oai on Rapa Nui. With ropes tied around the base, they needed the help of 16 other people to be able to move the sculpture from side to side in a situation similar to human footsteps. Later, Americans Terry Hunt and Carl Lipo confirmed the method by transporting the statue over 328 using the same practices.

Tourist on Easter Island

EASTER ISLAND NOWADAYS

The territory continues to receive tourists from all over the world. There are currently around 10,000 locals working directly with the local culture during the busiest times for visitors. The Moai statues function as a veritable open-air archaeological museum. For this reason, the best time to visit the island is in summer, especially in December, when the weather is sunny during the day and mild after dark. The volcanoes, which have been dormant for more than ten centuries, make up the region's landscape and serve as historical references for the guides. Many archaeologists also lead excursions to the site in search of traces of the techniques used to build the anthological stone sculptures.

The remaining heritage of the Rapa Nui civilization includes 670 Moai statues and 240 ceremonial temples. Each tour can be done by motorcycle, car, on horseback or walking. The distance from one end of the island to the other is 12.4 miles. In just four days, tourists can see all the important sites of the lost city.

To get to Easter Island, visitors have a few options from Brazil. From São Paulo, for example, travellers can take a bus or a direct flight to Santiago. From the Chilean capital, it is necessary to board another plane to the village of Hanga Roa, an inhabited place on the island with good landing conditions. There is only one flight option per day, which is usually very popular with tourists.

ARCHITECTURAL HERITAGE OF THE ANASAZI

4

WITH A TRAJECTORY FULL OF ADVANCES, THE PRIMITIVE AMERICAN INDIANS SUCCUMBED TO NATURAL PROBLEMS AND PRACTICES OF CANNIBALISM

Past tribes in religious rituals

The Anasazi Indians were the first inhabitants of what is now known as the "four corners" region in the United States. Comprising the states of Colorado, Utah, New Mexico and Arizona, the territory provided the social and cultural rise of the ancient civilization. Although they did not practice any activity related to writing techniques, they left impressive architectural traces by constructing buildings up to five stories high, considered giants in the daily life of the primitive era. Their main activities took place around 1200 BC, resulting in two monuments classified as UNESCO World Heritage Sites. In addition to construction related work, all the remains found show an indigenous daily life based on weaving, pottery, and irrigation techniques. Another highlight for the Anasazi was the development of roads to connect their villages. Although they were unaware of the wheel and the services of metallurgy, the system was 403 miles long and up to 19.7 feet wide in some sections.

FORMER ENEMIES

During the period of ascension, a group of inhabitants from the indigenous regions called the Pueblo people formed within the city. Evidence from the past does not reveal exactly what the ancient tribes called themselves. The name Anasazi means "ancient people" and was chosen by later societies to refer to their American ancestors. In the native language of the Indians, the name represents "ancient enemies". At its peak, the community

Monument of the Mesa Verde region in Colorado

contained more than 30,000 inhabitants divided between a large network of tribes constantly adopting influences from different cultures. Each location had independent leadership, but three villages stood out in the expansion of this civilization: Chaco Canyon, active in New Mexico, Kayenta, in northeastern Arizona, and San Juan, located in Colorado. The egalitarian way of life of these communities was extremely successful for over a thousand years through peace agreements between the villages. They depended above all on hunting animals, farming techniques and trading corn with neighbouring regions. The inhabitants became great experts in growing food, prioritizing rainfed practices, building dams to increase productivity, depending only on good weather conditions.

HISTORICAL ARCHITECTURE

Of all the buildings erected by the Anasazi Indians, only a few emblematic monuments remain in their original position. Archaeologists responsible for studying the territory are still at a loss to explain the usefulness of many of the houses, roads, towers, and stone complexes. The largest architectural spaces designed by the indigenous tribes were the houses built on the rocky wall of the Chaco Canyon in New Mexico. The urbanization area had about 30,031.56 square feet of canyons, plateaus, and hills in the middle of several villages with buildings that reached five floors distributed in 800 rooms.

Several American Indians claim to be descendants of the Anasa-

Housing towers built by the Anasazi

zi. Without historical proof, they call themselves Puebloans in reference to the ancient Pueblo people. Currently, they believe that the civilization of the past has not disappeared, but has simply migrated to the southwest, creating a new population of Native Americans. Little is known about whether there is historical continuity between the indigenous inhabitants of the United States. Some scholars argue that the link between the tribes is only geographical.

ADVANCED DESIGN

Around 750 BC, still in the early days of engineering, the Indians began to develop different architectural techniques. With peculiar methods related to the construction system, they erected monuments so high that they can only be accessed today by teams of climbers. As a result, the indigenous cities grew even more in terms of infrastructure. Among the buildings erected at this time were immense stone towers on the cliffs, circular observatories, and apartment complexes in the centres of the communities. Until the middle of the 19th century, these structures were considered the greatest engineering feats in North America.

The golden age of the Anasazi took place between 900 and 1150, when the cities began to house temples, mansions, and granaries. The whole structure was similar to that of large cosmopolitan areas. The buildings, including famous landmarks such as the Bandelier National Monument, were erected during this phase with cement mortars carved into the limestone. The increasingly urbanized centres welcomed pilgrims and traders from other regions. One of the great local attractions was the popular production of carpet sold by the indigenous peoples.

KACHINA BELIEF

The dwellings in the Pueblo complexes adopted an operating system known as Kiva. In approximately 60 circular rooms located in the giant towers, industrial centres specialized in weaving cotton. The large spaces also housed religious ceremonies of the ancestral culture based on the Kachina belief, involving the worship of spiritual beings and typical dances. Currently, several remaining tribes continue to practice the same rituals as their ancestors. The Ute, the Zuni, the Navajo, and the Hopi are supposedly Indians directly descended from the Anasazi. Most of the ancient city's activities involve a series of astronomical studies. Some researchers have concluded that ceremonial buildings located in Chaco Canyon also served as centres for learning about the cycles of the Moon, the Sun, and stellar conjunctions.

Various theories maintain that the Pueblo peoples built up a kind

Anasazi civilization monument in Cedar Mesa, Utah

of information network linked to knowledge about the science of the stars, attracting pilgrims from different parts of the American continent. In the middle of the 12th century, the most influential members of the civilization may have left in search of higher altitudes. The reasons that led them to abandon the site remain a great mystery to geologists. It is speculated that the natives fled worried about successive violent invasions of the region. For them, the ideal solution was to build dwellings in higher places to make it more difficult for their enemies to access them.

THE NATURAL ENVIRONMENT

Despite all the social upswing based on the production of abundant food, the American soil at the time did not have good conditions for agriculture. The region has been marked for centuries by arid climate conditions, which make much of the territory desert or semi-desert. Altitude problems also interfere with the survival system, causing extremely cold winters with snow covering the entire length of the land. The difference in temperature between the seasons also made animal husbandry and hunting difficult. The urbanizations culturally impacted by the Anasazi extended across the Colorado plateaus, interspersed with rivers and streams. The natural resources extracted from the soil include complex materials such as sandstone and volcanic rock. Accustomed to the climatic routine of the region, the inhabitants knew how to use all the setbacks to their advantage by planting cassava leaves and mastering different irrigation methods, even negotiating with regions of Mesoamerica, made up of areas linked to the south of present-day Mexico.

COMMERCIAL DIFFERENCES

Over the centuries, the growing exploitation of natural resources began to cause extended periods of drought in the territory. Even before the arrival of the Europeans, the population was going through periods of hardship. At this point, tribal divisions began to emerge based on monetary resources and leadership influence. Even though they were used to adverse situations, the Anasazi did not know how to deal with problems that were considered fatal. Faced with extreme climate change caused by excessive deforestation, natural resources became increasingly scarce. All the vegetation was cut down to build new homes as the population grew. Terrified, members of the elite isolated themselves to ensure that their way of life was not altered during what they considered to be just a crisis.

THEORIES OF EXTINCTION

As the civilization did not know how to write, it is practically impossible to say exactly why the Anasazi declined. Although the problems related to nature were overwhelming, many researchers claim that a succession of internal wars, initiated by the dispute over still existing natural resources, may have further increased the moment of chaos. Unbridled population growth and constant political impasses also had an influence on the migration process that took place at the time. However, the version most accepted by scholars refers to flaws in the region's ecosystem, caused by the exploitation of various areas of local nature. The last serious drought among indigenous tribes supposedly occurred in 1275, lasting a long 14 years. By the time the Spanish arrived in the American Southwest in the 16th century, there was no trace of the empire built up by the native Indians.

ANTHROPOPHAGY PRACTICES

University of California paleoanthropologist Timothy White has found evidence of cannibalistic activities among the inhabitants of the Mancos site, located on the Colorado-New Mexico border. Among men, women, and children, around 30 people were butchered and their remains prepared as a meal in clay containers. The act took place around the year 1200, possibly caused by internal conflicts aggravated by food shortages. Research has found burn marks on all parts of the bones,

Ancient drawings in the regions populated by the Anasazi Indians

including polishing on the ends caused by friction with the clay while they were being cooked. The Anasazi may have resorted to anthropophagy frequently in their final years.

INDIGENOUS ACTUALITY

Contemporary indigenous groups in the American territory believe it is impossible for the Anasazi to have abandoned their cities in the past. Considered heirs to their ancestral culture, they regularly undertake large expeditions to the states where the lost civilizations settled. The trips seek to better identify rituals and preserve the oral history of extinct peoples. The predominant characteristics of the Anasazi remain active through the dissemination of their culture and studies of the native language. Although there is no evidence to prove the links between the present-day tribes and the lost communities, their leaders preserve their history and are proud of their great advances. Testimonies from Spanish conquistadors have also contributed to important discoveries about the customs of the indigenous ancestors. Currently, the largest population of Amerindians are the Cherokees, who originated from the nation called the Iroquois.

THE RELIGIOUS VIOLENCE OF MOCHICA SOCIETY

5

TO MAINTAIN THE CONTROL AND HEGEMONY OF THEIR GOVERNMENT OVER THE PEOPLE, THE COMMANDERS OF THIS PERUVIAN CIVILIZATION CARRIED OUT CONSTANT RITUALS OF HUMAN SACRIFICE

Long before the Inca Empire dominated Peruvian territory, the Moche civilization, also known as the Mochica, occupied the region with artistic, religious, and bloody activities. With a system of leadership based on a centralized form of government, they emerged around 95 BC, in the Trujillo region, on the northern coast of Peru. Despite the unfavourable conditions, typical of the desert climate of the place, some researchers believe that the society managed to coexist for a long time amicably with the changes in nature. Extremely creative, the natives worked on the architectural development of the ancient city, building giant pyramids, considered historical monuments today. One of the most complex works is the Temple of the Sun, designed in homage to religious beliefs, with more than 50 million bricks. They were also wise metallurgists and pleased the nobility with their production of artifacts of copper and gold. Widely used in decorative pieces at the time, gold represented power and wealth in the traditions of the past.

FOOD VARIETY

Society was made up of several independent groups who faithfully shared the same cultural traditions. Land cultivation was one of the main sources of food production for the inhabitants, who used complex irrigation methods to grow potatoes, corn, and beans on a large scale. Veritable seafood feasts ensured different types of nutrients on the inhabitants' menu, providing energy to carry out their daily activities. Llamas served as a means of transportation and, in some situations,

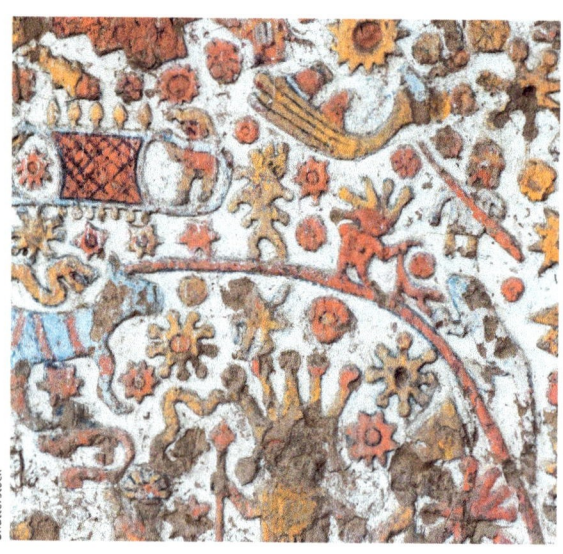

Details of narrative drawings made by the Mochica on a mural found in the Huaca de la Luna region

> **ORIGIN OF THE NAME**
> The Mochica were named after the Moche River, located in northern Peru. In 1899, German Max Uhle found the first evidence of the existence of civilization in this region. The name means "sanctuary" in the native Andean language, now extinct.

completed the meals. Even though they disappeared more than a thousand years before the first steps of the Inca leaders, many scholars consider the characteristics adopted by the Mochica to be the main influences that led the later society to build a powerful empire. As the desert climate prevailed for most of the year, water was valued as a precious item by the farmers, who depended on the rivers around the Andes to survive.

POLITICAL RELATIONS

Despite practicing so many advanced activities in a primitive age, the Moche did not master any writing techniques. Their main records were taken from drawings carved on pieces of pottery. Initially, all political and religious power was in the hands of a spiritual leader called Ai-Apaec. The figure of the ruler was seen as a kind of deity among the city's inhabitants, who held various worship services in his honour. In the middle of the year 50, the death of the leader led to the takeover by groups of priests active in warfare, known locally as Mochica lords. The new government founded a confederation that promptly transformed the entire 248 mile territorial extension into several nuclei of governmental states. Although they were equally strict with their enemies, the measures adopted by the lords brought many improvements to the population. During this period, the main Mochica community, located in the Moche River valley, reached 15,000 inhabitants. The administrative structure of the time prioritized military, religious, economic, and political domination. In many ways, the leadership of the priests can be compared to the administration of the pharaohs in ancient Egypt. The ostentatious decoration of the palaces and the belief in the afterlife of their sovereigns are the greatest similarities that identify the boundaries between religiosity and politics.

ARTISTIC WONDERS

With their meticulous techniques, the region's artisans were incredibly talented. They were the first in South America to use moulds in the process of making their works and inspired various contemporary

Ruins of Mochica society in Trujillo, Peru

methods of artistic study. Rigorously faithful to human traits, they told much of their history through the drawings depicted on their ceramic pieces. The Mochica style of production is currently called "huaco-portrait" within classical schools of art. The peculiar methodology emerged in the 5th century in the city of "Huaca de la Luna". The most popular are the elongated vases that show the daily life of the Moche inhabitants, including scenes of explicit sex. Although completely original, the society's ceramic utensils were influenced by the art produced by civilizations living in the Amazon and elsewhere in the Andes. Several experts classify the productions of the Andean community as the most beautiful works created in antiquity.

Most of the region's inhabitants occupied themselves with rural duties and, when the economy was doing well, they took advantage of the good times to produce artistic products, typical of the local people. The dry desert environment contributed to the construction of murals illustrating the main tasks carried out by the Moche in drawings that gave rise to various mythological stories. The dissemination of the products created by the artists initiated a large trade network, further expanding the conquests of the territory.

> Any gold artifact was valued as a rarity by the noble and powerful Mochica. To make everything they produced look golden, the region's artists would dip the copper items in a substance developed from the original gold mixed with small amounts of sodium bicarbonate and other salts.

RELIGIOUS BELIEFS

The Mochica mixed religious and political concepts. The figure of Ai-Apaec, considered the supreme god of all the natives, developed a doctrine inspired by dualistic nature. The leaders were responsible, in the people's view, for guaranteeing social order and the balance of material issues. To conquer spiritual powers and demonstrate his courage as a commander, Ai-Apaec took part in a bloody battle against a puma. According to Andean culture, the wild animal represented all the impure feelings that caused disorder in the world. In traditional rituals, the ruler had to consume human blood so that his strength would multiply and he could win the battle. Sacrificial offerings were made with the blood of prisoners captured during invasions of other lands after a long period of torture. Later rulers lived like true deities. During rituals in the cities, the subjects would spread mercury sulphate on the ground so that the rulers would not step directly on the ground. The hierarchy of the Moche was defined by the absolute rule of the king, followed by the authority of the priests and, lastly, the military guards.

VIOLENT RITUALS

Mochica cultural traditions included various sacrificial ceremonies. One of the most curious is related to the appearance of the atmospheric phenomenon El Niño, which promoted real massacres. All the violence instituted in the community's routine increased the power of the leaders and increasingly intimidated the common population. The religious philosophy of the time preached that the only way to contain the drastic climate changes typical of the region was to offer human blood as a sacrifice. While El Niño remained active, the Mochica were frightened by the frequency of torrential rains and floods. For every situation, there was a ritual of homage or worship to the deities of nature represented by the sovereigns. Warfare between the cities of the territory took place in the desert, with the defeated being displayed in chains in the public square before being tortured for several days in sacrificial temples in a secret location. The prisoner was beheaded by the leaders and then his blood was saved for consumption and offering work. However, all the hegemony of the Mochica power began to disappear around the year 500.

MYTHOLOGICAL DECLINE

As was the case with practically all the peoples who occupied the Peruvian Andes region, scholars find it very difficult to prove the historical events of the Mochica. Little is known to date about the reasons for the disappearance of this metropolis, which has resulted in a succession of legends handed down over the years. The main evidence was found in 1955 by American archaeologist Steve Bourget, in the territorial extension of Huaca de la Luna. Thousands of bones were catalogued over two months after the excavations to identify the movements practiced in the rituals and thus uncover how the inhabitants spent their last years. It seems that long rainy seasons, extremely rare in the desert, heralded the arrival of El Niño. There were more than three decades of daily flooding on the coast, followed by another 30 years of drought. The scarcity of resources further increased the violence among the Mochica who now, in addition to rituals, duelled over the few remaining spaces on the ground. Over time, the sacrifices began to be discredited by civilization, since the offerings did not prevent the climatic tragedies. Many priests were even murdered during this period for failing to save their lands. By the end of the 8th century, the last cities in the region were abandoned, ending the supremacy of the Moche.

THE AKKADIANS' METEORIC RISE

6

DOMINANT PART OF THE FIRST EMPIRE OF MESOPOTAMIA, THE CIVILIZATION CREATED THE MODEL OF CITY-STATES IN JUST TWO CENTURIES OF EXISTENCE

The history of the Akkadian people is directly linked to the social influence conquered by the Sumerians, known as humanity's first civilization. Around 2250 BC, tribes of nomads from the desert region of Syria invaded the territory that had belonged to Sumer until then. With difficulties in commercial expansion in their homeland, the immigrants were looking for an environment that offered better natural resources to develop a new civilization. The two armies fought bloody battles for every piece of the city. Despite having a fully developed culture operating from a metropolis system, Sumerian politics collapsed in the face of its own internal disorganization. Extremely vain commanders and long stalemates over war strategies facilitated the Akkadians' victory. In a short time, the troops dominated large urbanized centres in the region, spreading new religious and social customs among the inhabitants.

STATE MODEL

After the arrival of the sovereign of the city of Uruk, Lugal-zage-si, in 2375 BC, the two populations began to live together harmoniously in most villages, being unified by political decisions. With extremely similar beliefs and objectives, they formed Mesopotamia's first empire. From 2330 BC onwards, the region's government program developed important city-state models. Led by King Sargon I, the growth of the Semitic administrative model transformed the territory of Akkad into the capital of the ancient empire. The geographical extension, which today belongs to Iraq, and the city of Akkad are the main reasons for the

Illustration of inhabitants of the Mesopotamian empire on the Tigris River

name officially given to the ancient civilization, also known as Sumero-Akkadian. Each space was used as a way of contemplating the gods, transforming men into mere instruments to serve them. The entire cultural structure of society was based on the construction of temples and palaces.

RELIGIOUS PRACTICES

Living around polytheistic beliefs, the Akkadians worshipped various gods and animals as supreme beings in a series of religious rituals. The figure of the king was considered a kind of divinity, and even after his death the devotion of the subjects remained intact. Even though they dominated most of the territory, some Akkadian leaders still paid taxes to Sumerians who owned important villages in the cities. The agreement guaranteed the peaceful coexistence of the peoples, dividing power and influence in the organization of community affairs. With the progress made by the ancient metropolis model, the region ruled by the empire came to cover the entire Mediterranean Sea and Anatolia.

UNIVERSAL REIGN

Taking care of the entire administrative structure of the cities, the king dominated political and institutional affairs. The system was based on a centralized state, and the people participated in military convocations to defend their empire. The ruler was considered by the inhabitants to be a direct descendant of the gods and was elected king of the entire universe. Many Sumerian activities were preserved during the empire, such as offering the construction of temples, called ziggurats, and agricultural work to the gods. The food produced represented a large part of the Akkadian economy, helped by the region's climate and the flooding of the Tigris and Euphrates rivers. As there was no form of currency at the time, barley was widely used to obtain products that were difficult to find in the region. Advanced water resource techniques were also part of the inhabitants' daily lives. They stored water for possible periods of drought and learned to take advantage of floods near rivers. They created around 12 city-states in the territory, including Quish, Nipur and Lagash.

URBAN REVOLUTION

All the areas of the city-states had special stretches set aside solely for agricultural cultivation. Each pole stood out from the other urban centres and was controlled by priests in partnership with groups of elders respected by the nobility in the territory.

The commanders of the areas favourable to agriculture were called "pastesi" and received various social duties from the monarch leaders, such as collecting taxes, organizing the residents of the communities, controlling the activities of the army, administering the temples, and overseeing the construction of hydraulic works. Everything related to the land was done freely by the inhabitants since, according to religious traditions, the property belonged to the gods worshipped by all. The development of cuneiform writing by the Sumerians allowed Akkadian traders to sell products to other civilizations and to develop a vast literary production full of mythologies over the centuries.

CONFLICTING INVASIONS

Around 2150 BC, the society of the Akkadians began to be dismantled. Their period of activity (two centuries) was relatively short compared to other lost civilizations. Located in a territory favourable to the flourishing of natural resources, they suffered several invasion attempts during their heyday. Armed with weapons considered advanced in the historical context of that time, their leaders developed military techniques used in conflicts against peoples from other regions. Although they were fully prepared to defend their lands, they were unable to withstand the attacks constantly organized by the nomadic Gutis. Coming from Armenia, the Asians took advantage of the political weakness among the Akkadians after the death of King Sargon I. His death brought about a serious power crisis in the community, leading to several internal revolts. The invaders formed a strong strategic scheme to dominate all the cities of the Mesopotamian Empire. In addition to the difficult political situation, the successive invasions weakened the leaders of the territory. Only the city of Ur managed to stand up to the Gutis warriors and survive the domination attempt. By the year 2000 BC, practically the entire region built by the Akkadians had been taken over by the Elamite peoples.

BABYLONIAN EMPIRE

Among the invaders of Mesopotamia, the most historically notable were the Amorite groups. Originating in the Arabian desert, they took part in a series of battles until they settled in the city of Babylon, in the region of Middle Mesopotamia. Around the 18th century BC, King Hammurabi formed the first Babylonian empire, unifying all the city-states in the territory. In a short time, the place became an influential urban centre, known for its advanced architectural constructions. The civilization is mentioned in the Bible for having erected the Ziggurat of Babel, designed as a tower to take the

THE AKKADIANS' METEORIC RISE

Tower of Babel, historical monument mentioned in Bible supposedly located between the Tigris rivers and Euphrates, in Mesopotamia, where the society of the Akkadians lived

inhabitants to heaven. They lived with a strict penal code in which the policy of "an eye for an eye, a tooth for a tooth" was established, causing countless crimes motivated by revenge and personal interests. Under the command of Emperor Nebuchadnezzar II, society conquered the Hebrew people and the city of Jerusalem. After an invasion organized by the Persians, in 539 BC the territory was dominated by the strong army commanded by the legendary king Cyrus, known as The Great in his homeland.

> The first document recorded as a penal constitution was written in the Akkadian language, based on the cuneiform script that was once used throughout the Middle East. Drafted in the Amorite state after the demise of the Sumero-Akkadian empire, it was named the Code of Hammurabi after the Babylonian king of the same name. The set of laws was active around 1772 BC and was found by archaeological expeditions in 1901 in the Mesopotamian region.

ASSYRIAN WARRIORS

Another important civilization in Mesopotamia was the Assyrians. Emerging after the end of the first phase of Babylonian rule, they acted according to the laws of the code developed by the region's former ruler. Subordinated to the king's authority, they lived practically in slavery, being sold as merchandise along with their land and owing respect to the dominant villages. Among the most important cities at the time were Nineveh, Assur, and Nimrod, all of which obeyed the administrative rules of the territory. The ruler was considered a deity among humans and therefore kept as much distance as he could from the population. Fearful of religious beliefs, the monarch practiced extensive fasts and only spoke to important figures in the palace. The local army, considered cruel and ruthless, had very modern technologies for that period, such as the use of iron in their weapons and copper. In their heyday, they controlled Cyprus, Egypt and all the cities of Mesopotamia. Invasions by various peoples and the independence of Egypt contributed to the demise of this civilization, which had major administrative flaws. The Chaldeans took the city of Nineveh, putting an end to all the remaining cultures of the Babylonian empire.

Ruins located in the Assyrian region

Signs used in cuneiform writing

LEARN ABOUT CUNEIFORM WRITING

Developed by the Sumerians, signs began to be used around 3500 B.C. Extremely enigmatic in their early days, writing symbols are represented by drawings of wedge-shaped objects. The population usually wrote on clay tablets or plaques, which disappeared over time. For permanent texts, they took the pieces to ovens, marking the records. The cuneiform alphabet had more than 2,000 signs, making the work of researchers even more difficult when it came to deciphering them.

Initially, only the most influential members of society, such as nobles, priests, and landowners, learned to communicate through writing. The common people acquired the technique as economic and commercial needs arose. The resource helped in the administration of property records, sales calculations, the increase of plantations and the inheritance of valuable artifacts.

Over time, people throughout Mesopotamia mastered cuneiform writing, recording their work routines and even some thoughts in the form of a diary. The expansion of the technique resulted in several changes to the original style, so that everyone could learn it. However, the humblest inhabitants found it very difficult to understand the signs.

In the middle of the 20th century, the first records were found proving the existence of cuneiform writing. To decipher them, they needed a large team that was also fluent in Hebrew and Arabic. The translation was carried out by combining the similarities found between the signs of all the languages. The inhabitants of Mesopotamia, at different times, left the largest number of historical records of writing, proving the importance of the technique in their civilization.

TIWANAKU'S AGRICULTURAL EMPIRE

7

AMONG THOUSANDS OF ARCHAEOLOGICAL REMAINS, ANDEAN SOCIETY REVEALS MUCH OF ITS SUCCESSFUL HISTORY, WHICH LASTED MORE THAN FIVE CENTURIES

Porta do Sol monument, that represents the solar calendar.

Considered one of the main civilizations of ancient South America, the city of Tiwanaku is impressive for having cultivated a series of historical achievements over the centuries. Located near Lake Titicaca, the territory covers a large geographical expanse 44.64 miles from La Paz. The starting point is centred in southern Peru, encompassing the Bolivian Andes and skirting neighbouring parts of Chile. Popularly known as a powerful agricultural empire, the society began its activities around 400 BC, reaching its peak between 500 and 900 BC. Today there are only ruins of important monuments on the site, which contributes to the emergence of legends about how the inhabitants of the community lived. With a very efficient administrative system, Tiwanaku was the longest-running metropolis on the continent, lasting more than 500 years. One of the most admired characteristics of this people is their extensive creativity in architectural and engineering construction. The entire remaining area of the archaeological site has been a UNESCO World Heritage Site since 2000 and is administered by the Bolivian authorities.

MORAL CONCEPTS

The formation of the empire played a significant role in influencing later Andean cities. Guided by strong moral concepts, the civilization built a successful cultural and political metropolis. They transformed the hardships of the region's arid plateau into fields of fertile soil, ensuring a balanced economy. The terraces shaped for plantations favoured the growth of agriculture with constant and large-scale production. With an estimated population between 30 and 40 thousand people, Tiwanaku was a large administrative centre dominated by centralized power. In addition to public buildings, the inhabitants also created ingenious solutions to the water problems they faced during periods of prolonged drought, alternating with storms that lasted for days. Around the main monument erected at the time, the pyramid of Akapana, researchers found several functional channels for the flow of water straight from the river during periods of flooding.

RENOWNED ASTRONOMERS

Great scholars of cosmology, they even developed a renowned reference centre on the subject, receiving pilgrimages of researchers from various places. Many archaeologists claim that it is practically impossible to define an exact number for the population of Tiwanaku, given that the resources taken from the fertile soil supported practically all the native families and many visitors, who ended up staying permanently. The community's administrative system also produced copper in order to gain advantages in military confrontations. In its period of expansion, the civilization used its independence in food production and territorial advantages to sign trade agreements with the members of the colonies. Without technological aids, they believed they were at the centre of the Earth. Some mythological sto-

Ruins of the Tiwanaku archaeological site

ries say that the inhabitants of the community lived for around 120 years. The secret to their longevity lay in their diet, which was full of meat, potatoes, and fish.

IMPACFTUL CONSTRUCTIONS

Adopting a peculiar style of architecture and engineering, the inhabitants of the region have created true megalithic monuments. For more than five centuries, the administrative capital of Tiwanaku designed buildings with extremely orderly and meticulously carved stones. Among the main ruins remaining on the site are the Puma Punku, Kantatalitta and Kerikala pyramids. Many scholars believe that the civilization created the first model South American state. The poor condition of the archaeological site led the Bolivian government to begin a long process of restoring the historic area. Although they have followed the architectural features suggested by the traces left by the original buildings, it is not known whether the new monuments are exactly faithful to the Tiwanaku style. The restoration process has been hampered by the fact that there are no concrete records of the first studies in the area. The degradation of the ruins was caused by countless lootings, carried out in search of precious artifacts during amateur excavations, since the decline of the population. From the beginning of the 20th century, the decommissioned territory served as a firing range for military teams. The deteriorated state of the rocks is also due to the construction of a railroad during the same period. Most of the buildings in Tiwanaku were built randomly, with similar blocks, designed to suit different situations. Only once the construction was finished was its usefulness defined for the inhabitants. The researchers' work was made even more difficult by the numerous changes to the names of the city's sites. In addition to the archaeological park, which is open to visitors, the region also now has lithic and ceramics museums.

ARTISTIC REMAINS

Like most ancient peoples, the inhabitants of Tiwanaku told much of their routine through sculptures scattered throughout the territory and artistic ceramics. Bennett's monolith, currently located in the city's lithic museum, is seven meters high and weighs around 44,100 pounds. The sculpture is considered the largest anthropomorphic piece remaining from all Andean cultures. Little is known about the monument's real significance. Some believe it to be an ancient warrior. The more religious claim that it is a tribute to the goddess Pachamama, one of the daughters of the sovereign deity in Tiwanaku, known as the creator Viracocha. The statue makes references to various themes related to the community's daily life, such as agriculture, astronomy, and fish farming. In one hand, the monolith is holding a kind of symbol of political power, representing the social leaders and priests of the region. In the museums of Tiwanaku, there are several sculptures with multiple heads and other monuments structured in gigantic rocks. The artistic ceramics showed human features with oriental characteristics.

RELIGIOUS RITUALS

The beliefs held by the people of Tiwanaku revolve around the deity Viracocha, also known as Huiracocha. According to religious concepts, the spiritual being is considered the great master of the world, responsible for the creation of people and all things linked to nature. Rituals in his honour were directly related to the flowering of the crops and the changing of the seasons. Only the nobles and city leaders took part in the events, believing that these were intellectual studies that would be difficult for the humble peasants to understand. The mythology established by the doctrine divided the universe into three parts: the upper world, in which there were divine and celestial beings, the present world, made up of human beings, and the subterranean world, the destination of the souls of deceased ancestors. Statues were built to illuminate the different spheres. The men functioned as liaisons between the will of the gods and the direction of society. Religious theories say that Viracocha emerged from the waters of the Titicaca River and created the sky, the earth and all the existing elements. In various legends, the deity appears with only four fingers holding a snake in his hands. The religious belief was preserved, in different forms, by most of the later Andean civilizations.

PASSAGE OF TIME

The Kalasasaya temple is home to one of the greatest icons related to Tiwanaku culture. The Sun Gate is supposedly located in a strategic position that has aligned the solar calendar in the city for over 11,000 years. Today, the monument built with volcanic remains is three meters high and weighs more than 28,665 pounds. As well as the figure of Viracocha, the sculpture also includes 48 other drawings symbolizing animal shapes. The locals usually celebrate the arrival of the New Year Solstice, which begins in winter, around June 21, in front of the iconic stone block. The Moon Gate, represented in the region as one of the elements that determine the passage of time, is also linked to various rites of passage according to the alignment of its phases. As the society did not have any form of writing, it is even more difficult to confirm the theories involved about their beliefs and rituals.

FINAL MOMENTS

The events that led to Tiwanaku's extinction took place long before the arrival of the Spanish colonizers in the region. In the middle of the 11th century, the society was known as a strong center of administration, renowned in the metallurgical and astronomical sectors. Although they found ingenious solutions to deal with the difficulties caused by the region's arid geography, they succumbed to drastic climatic changes. According to groups of archaeologists, the waters of Lake Titicaca receded, causing serious deficiencies in agriculture. In such situations, the altitude brings even more problems of thermal amplitude, with intense heat during the day and extreme cold at dusk. Faced with these changes, the soil has been completely disconfigured by the successive aggressions of rains and low temperatures combined with prolonged droughts. Although strong evidence links the extinction of the civilization to climatic chaos, the causes of the disappearance of the Tiwanaku empire remain a mystery.

Tiwanaku archaeological site details

VIKING SOCIETY'S CONQUESTS

8

THE NORDIC WARRIORS BECAME FAMOUS AFTER A SERIES OF INVASIONS THAT SPREAD FEAR AND TERROR ACROSS EUROPEAN TERRITORIES DURING THE 10TH CENTURY

Frequent protagonists in various literary and cinematic stories, the Vikings continue to arouse curiosity in the contemporary world. The inhabitants of ancient Nordic Greenland developed a powerful society that spread fear and terror wherever it went. Among their many conquests, the colonies formed in other countries after bloody battles stand out. Coming from northern Europe on the Scandinavian Peninsula, the Vikings dominated the Arctic territory in 980 during an unusual period of favourable weather on the island. Without establishing any kind of official economic regime, the inhabitants used their agricultural produce as currency to survive. The laws of coexistence were based on violence and conservatism. All punishments were severely applied to the people, causing long inquisitorial seasons, including executions by bonfire. Any argument, regardless of its origin, could be resolved with physical duels, causing bloodbaths between the villages of the city. As well as being excellent warriors, the Vikings were also traders, pirates, navigators, workers, and farmers.

VIOLENT EXPEDITIONS

Between the 7th and 11th centuries, maritime groups formed by the Vikings travelled in search of vulnerable territories to carry out looting and colonizing activities. Their ships gained fame for the menacing decorations placed on their prows as a way of intimidating their opponents. The most feared was the head of an animal that, from a distance, resembled the features of a dragon, earning the boats used in the voyages the nickname drakkars. Proficient in advanced construction systems, the Vikings designed vessels that were very different from those existing at the time. Fast, they were essential for surprising the population of invaded territories. Their aggressive personality prevented any attempt by their opponents to flee or react. In a series of violent expeditions, the Norse colonized the entire sea coast of Scandinavia, some areas of Russia, the north-eastern Baltic Sea, parts of England, the coast of Portugal, Spain, Italy, Sicily, and areas of Palestine. Despite so many geographical conquests, the best-known attack carried out by the Vikings was against the Byzantine Empire, in the capital Constantinople, in 907. At the time, the invading army had 80,000 men and more than 2,000 ships.

VIKING ROUTINE

Their diet was practically based on items obtained through fishing, trading with other villages and maritime commerce. Extremely creative, they built houses, farms, churches and designed complex weapons of war. Everything was reproduced according to the lifestyle previously known in Europe. Around the year 1000 they reached their peak living in the Arctic region, encouraging the arrival of three other fleets of compatriots on the island. The administrative system was divided between fiefdoms control-

Illustration of the viking invasions published in Voyage Journal between 1800 and 1801

led by sovereign leaders and power centralized in the figure of a king. During the warmer days, they hunted marine animals, cut wood, produced dairy products by raising cattle and stored bales of hay. One of the main forms of trading took place when European vessels passed the island and exchanged luxury artifacts or foods specific to each region. Religious items such as wine, rosaries, silver, and jewellery were exported from Norway to be worn by the most influential members of society. To withstand the harsh winter, they worked on restoration activities in the buildings, drew up architectural plans, established methods to preserve crops and increase profits from foreign trade. Other important transactions were made with polar bear skins, silk, and Baltic amber.

FEARED MEN

The violent practices of Viking warriors led the European authorities of the time to build veritable fortresses around their lands. Various security measures were adopted in strategic locations, such as ports, churches and castles inhabited by the monarchy of each territory. The Arctic invaders were so feared that many religious groups published specific prayers asking for protection from the Viking bloodbaths. According to Nordic tradition, the inheritance left by the head of the family after his death was passed on directly to the eldest son. The other descendants had to find alternative activities to enrich themselves. At the time, the main way to gain wealth was to take part in maritime expeditions that plundered other countries. The Viking army's total lack of fear frightened their opponents. Legendary vessels of the civilization, such as the Knorr ships, were around 65.62 feet long, 16.40 feet wide and carried up to 70 people. With advanced warfare strategies, the invaders laid siege to several cities on the continent, taking advantage of important climatic factors to gain the upper hand. When they surprised their victims, they made maximum use of the structure of their ships, which were designed to withstand strong storms without suffering too many tremors.

RELIGIOUS CUSTOMS

For most of their existence, the Vikings adopted polytheistic practices, worshipping several gods. The most popular was the chief god Odin, considered the main mythological figure of Norse religiosity. Thor, god of thunder and battles, was highly worshipped before the famous invasions. Another spiritual being of great significance to the community was the goddess of fertility, known as Freya. In drawings created by the population, the female figure was depicted wearing a kind of magical necklace with elements attributed to an earthly deity. According to legendary cultural stories, each spiritual being lived in a place called Asgard, forming a parallel reality. The space was linked to earthly events by the Bifrost bridge, made up of a rainbow. The final judgment of the Norse people was scheduled to take place after a stratospheric battle that would destroy all the deities, resulting in a universal flood.

Completely faithful to their beliefs, the Vikings resisted the ascendant Catholic customs throughout Europe for a long time. During their journeys in search of slaves and vulnerable territories to steal precious materials, they always targeted properties belonging to the clergy as the main targets of their invasions. Over the years, however, it became impossible not to incorporate Catholicism, and they were the last European population to adopt the religion's customs. Frightened by the constant attacks, representatives of the church described the Vikings to the Catholics as barbaric, dangerous, and rude men. Some monks even classified the warriors as a way for God to punish the population that suffered their attacks. The entry of many Viking groups into Catholicism was also due to commercial interests, signing agreements for territories.

ECONOMIC CLASSES

Society was divided between representatives of the nobility, powerful elite farmers, and humble peasants. A large part of the population lived in simple one-room dwellings. The houses of the wealthier members of the community had living rooms, bedrooms, bathrooms, and kitchens. All the buildings were made from the same base: wood, stone, and dry grass. The administration of the family, according to Nordic customs, was centred on the father figure. Regardless of their economic class, all the men took part in the meetings organized by the town leaders with the aim of defining social issues and punishing the inhabitants who committed any crime.

SOCIAL DIVISION

Women's role was restricted to caring for their houses and children. Although very modest, some female tribes colonized in European countries allowed women to wear clothes that were considered extravagant for the time. If they were not slaves, Viking girls were allowed to marry at the age of 12. Although they were still very young, the custom allowed them to ask for a divorce, inherit their husband's property and have their dowries returned. Special care was also taken to pass on the main local stories and traditions to the children. The commanders believed that this could be a way of preventing the community from being lost if the warriors were killed in a conflict. The concern extended to the members of their colonies conquered in other countries. Practically the entire population used stone and metal materials to keep warm in winter. Due to the Nordic climate, it was necessary to combine leather garments and thick animal skins. Blonde hair was seen as an ideal of beauty. Vikings were usually born swarthy and were easily impressed by the physical features of native opponents from other parts of Europe. Some colonies used soaps with a high caustic soda content to lighten hair and beards.

RED WARRIOR

One of the main characters in Viking culture was the leader Erik, known as "The Red" or "The Redhead". Before landing in Greenland, the people occupied parts of Norway, Sweden, and Denmark. Upon arriving on the Nordic Island, considered the largest in the world, the warrior was impressed by the size of the green area and named the territory after the predominance of natural features. Accompanying the commander, another 25 ships with around 500 people set sail, but only 15 vessels managed to reach their destination. Fleeing a murder charge against a superior, Erik managed to settle in the new land with his son. According to mythology, the quarrel occurred after his rival had killed a slave. During the duel, Erik took advantage of his enemy's weakness and killed him with axe blows, splitting his body into six parts. The story spread, making the leader feared by the entire population. Among the most popular figures in the legendary Viking story is also the group of Berserk warriors. Seized by an uncontrolled rage, they frightened their opponents and hardly ever lost a battle. It was a kind of supernatural transformation, known in mythology as rabid dogs. Some theories argue that the warriors' frightened reaction was due to the use of hallucinogenic mushrooms planted in the villages, especially amanita music.

CLIMATE CHANGE

The population of Nordic warriors lived peacefully in Greenland until the year 1100. A great season of exorbitant cold extended across the region for around 80 years after that. While they tried to adapt to the new temperature conditions, the inhabitants struggled to keep their crops alive with the constant attacks on the soil. Even the smallest climatic changes affected the storage of hay and the amount of ice concentrated in the sea. With shorter summers and increasingly icy days, the Vikings' trade was compromised, leading to a period of decline in agricultural production. The ice advanced so far in the region that it ended up isolating the civilization, preventing the arrival of sea vessels. Natural resources practically disappeared. Faced with a scarcity of wood, the inhabitants of the area used firewood accompanied by the remains of charcoal to heat water and other foodstuffs. In the process of extinction, society also suffered from the force of the winds, which made farming difficult. Activities considered common in the Vikings' daily lives disappeared, making it impossible to produce food. As a last resort, the population fed on animals grown for trade. Even hunting dogs were served as food. Around 1400, the entire structure of the Nordic empire was wiped out, and its inhabitants died of hunger and cold.

CULTURAL BLOCKADE

Adopting a completely conservative stance, the Norse prevented information about territorial neighbours from entering their community. On the other side of the island, in an unexplored part, lived tribes of Eskimos, known as Inuit. Adapted to the region's freezing cold, they produced a vast diet based on seal and whale meat. As a means of heating, the inhabitants used animal fat and the entire architectural structure of the society was built of ice sculptures, houses, and villages. It is speculated that two other populations settled in different parts of Nordic Greenland. In around 2500 BC, the Saqqaq built communities on the island until a sudden change in temperature destroyed all the soil. The survivors ended up leaving the area in 850 B.C. The Dorset found the region shortly after the decline of the Saqqaq, but also succumbed to the difficulties of feeding themselves in an area covered by glaciers. Today, the country receives many tourists offering a range of natural

Representation of a Viking warrior with a horned helmet

wonders, such as the aurora borealis and the midnight sun (when it remains daylight for 24 hours), whale watching and, of course, the ruins of the city built by the Vikings.

LOST CIVILIZATIONS IN THE AMAZON RAINFOREST

9

PRESERVING MYTHOLOGICAL STORIES OVER THE CENTURIES, THE ANCIENT PEOPLES OF THE REGION ACHIEVED GREAT ARTISTIC ADVANCES AND LEFT A PRECIOUS LEGACY IN SOUTH AMERICA

Among legends known the world over and facts that are relevant to archaeologists, the past of the Brazilian Amazon surprises with every discovery. The region is home to a series of cultures built in unfavourable situations for the population, in the face of a hostile climate and wild forests. Located in the heart of the Amazon Basin, the most advanced lost civilizations in the national territory developed countless solutions to grow in soil poor in nutrients but abundant in natural resources. Around 7 million indigenous people settled in the area, trading with other communities, discovering artistic techniques and providing innovative methods of agricultural production. Society functioned through the work of two predominant groups: the tribes of Tapajônica, located in the region of Santarém, now part of the state of Pará, and the Marajoara Indians, originally from the island of Marajó. After the arrival of the Europeans in the 16th century, the populations left valuable legacies, creating a peculiar mythology.

TERRA PRETA OR BLACK EARTH

Priests and friars who arrived in the region with the colonizing expeditions wrote diaries reporting on the main characteristics of the local civilizations. It is believed that the population of the past managed to live in the territory causing as little damage as possible to the natural reserves and the soil. Although their diet was centred on fish, the indigenous people were aware of the possibility of causing the extinction of species if they always hunted the same marine animals. The few impacts recorded were caused by deforestation in some parts of the forest to build the huts where the natives lived, around the rivers. River management systems were developed to help the water flow during flood seasons.

Originally, the land in the region did not offer good conditions for agricultural workers. The Amazonian soil was poor in nutrients, which reduced the variety of food. Using ingenious techniques, the tribes created "terra preta" by chemically altering the land. The process was carried out using organic waste, mixed with charcoal and broken pieces of pottery. The famous substance, preserved to this day by contemporary Indians, transformed the region into one of the most fertile areas for plantations recorded in Brazil.

SUPREMACY OF TAPAJÔNICA TRIBES

For more than 500 years, the Tapajônica tribes exerted a great influence throughout the Amazon territory. The villages were made up of Indians of Tupuliçus origin, who used weapons to intimidate their opponents in the region. Constant wars were waged to dispute control of the communities. One of the main methods of attack used by the

Indians consisted of a poison taken from vines. The substance, which was shot at enemies with arrows, would kill a human being in less than 24 hours. The state of sovereignty of the Tapajós was also consolidated with the exacerbated growth of the native population, winning all battles against neighbouring groups. Researchers indicate the possibility that the leaders of the Tapajós societies centralized all local power, promoting trade with distant villages and bringing together tribes of different ethnicities and languages.

HISTORICAL CERAMICS

The greatest evidence of the tribes' routines has been found thanks to the traces left by their legendary ceramic pieces. The work, admired worldwide, told stories in minutely detailed drawings. To produce the pieces, the Indians used clay and a river sponge called cauixi. Specialized artisans from the community shaped the objects by hand, ensuring a wealth of detail in delicate pieces. According to legends spread over the years, the ceramic utensils decorated important rituals, such as religious events and funerals. The Tapajós mixed the ashes of their dead relatives with juices made from corn or with substances taken from plants characteristic of the Amazon rainforest. The civilization's traditional urns have gained fame in archaeological studies. The bodies went through a system of embalming before entering the container. The final stage consisted of crushing the bones, which were served as tea and offered to all the members of the tribe in a kind of traditional bowl, considered very advanced for the artistic creations of the time. In the face of European exploitation, native culture gradually lost its main characteristics. The influence of the native leaders during their heyday stretched approximately 373 miles between the Amazon and Tapajós rivers.

MARAJOARA COMMUNITY

The archaeological site on the island of Marajó is home to the remains of large buildings built by the population in the past. With all the peculiarities common to large metropolises, the villages managed agricultural activities, based on the cultivation of manioc and traditional wild rice (arroz-bravo). The artistic style of this community was centred on the production of ceremonial ceramics. Various snakes were often depicted on the utensils. Each piece had a wide range of colours, hollow edges, different modelling, and incision techniques. The period of civilization's greatest advance took place between the 5th and 14th centuries. Another dominant characteristic of the Marajoara was their creativity in building huge embankments, which served as the starting point for the development of the entire architectural structure of the villages.

As the area was constantly flooded by rivers and rain, the buildings also helped to protect the residents. The residential spaces were built in places that could comfortably house up to a thousand people. The villages of this community covered an area of 7,720 square miles. During floods, the Indians could only get in and out of their villages in canoes built with resources taken from the environment.

EUROPEAN DESTRUCTION

The Marajoara population disappeared around 1300. The conditions that led to the decline of the civilization remain a mystery to this day. Archaeologists speculate that the extinction occurred after constant fighting between the villages, preventing the formation of defense strategies against attacks from other peoples. When the first Portuguese arrived in the region, there were no longer any native tribes. In their records, the European invaders also found no descendants of the Marajoara among the remaining Indians. Throughout their existence, they left their daily stories marked only in ceramic artwork, without mastering any writing technique. The pieces had drawings of animals common in the Amazon, such as scorpions, snakes, and lizards. The Tapajônica culture, on the other hand, disappeared as a result of exploitation by the colonizers. Since the first records of the Portuguese in Santarém, around 1661, the history of the oldest Indians in the territory has been told orally by residents of the archaeological site. Even after so many excavations and geographical surveys in the region, only a small amount of artistic pottery produced by the Tapajós has been found.

PALEOLITHIC PERIOD

Another Brazilian prehistoric culture had emerged during the Paleolithic period, in the vicinity of the Amazon Basin. Recent discoveries have contradicted the opinion of scientists who have always claimed that it would be very difficult to survive in closed and hostile jungle conditions, as is the case with the local vegetation. As the volume of the rivers could cover up the plantations in flood seasons, farming and hunting activities would be interrupted and the population would end up starving. American Anna Roosevelt, a professor at the University of Illinois, found traces that prove the existence of this ancient civilization in several excavations carried out at an archaeological site in Monte Alegre, in the municipality of Belém, in the state of Pará. Inside the Pedra Pintada cave, famous in the region for its historical content, they reported evidence that man lived there more than 11,200 years ago. Many red painted drawings record the characteristics of these people, such as images of local plants and animals. What is most impressive is the art related to human biological conditions. On the hills in the area, tourists must climb a series of rocks to find illustrations of women in labour and male and female reproductive organs.

ARTISTIC REMAINS

Despite many discoveries, it has not yet been possible to scientifically prove the existence of this ancient civilization of Monte Alegre. In addition to the drawings recorded in caves, the research also found pieces of pottery. Divided between gourds and vases, the artifacts are around 7600 years old. The studies of the material are looking for evidence of a technologically advanced culture, responsible for initiating the techniques still used today by art schools and remaining tribes in the Amazon Rainforest. The works were sculpted in clay and decorated by skilled hands to create realistic details. It is speculated that the community functioned as a large metropolis, compared to contemporary cities. 11,000 years ago, the region may have had around 300,000 inhabitants, five times more than the municipality's current population. Primitive humans adopted a diet rich in nutrients, prioritizing the consumption of meat. Bone remains found prove that animals of various species were charred. The main records show birds, bats, snakes, turtles, fish, frogs, rodents, and large wild mammals. It is not yet known how this society could have disappeared. Research in the region continues to look for traces of Brazil's Amazonian past.

MYTHOLOGICAL "EL DORADO"

Of all the legends born in the Amazon, the myth of "El Dorado" is the most popular worldwide. The theory, which continues to be disseminated over the centuries, describes the existence of a lost city in the labyrinths of the Brazilian jungle. The dream of finding this mystical territory has led many researchers to venture into the jungles in search of supposed lands filled with gold. The rumours were so intense during the Portuguese colonization that the myth of "El Dorado" spread to various parts of Europe. The version told by the South Americans describes the routine of a very wealthy leader who covered himself from head to toe in gold to demonstrate his power every morning. After nightfall, the ruler bathed in a sacred lake in order to remove the elements from his body. In this interpretation, "El Dorado" did not represent a place; the story only featured a symbolic figure. The most accepted explanation, according to scholars, is that it was all an invention by the indigenous tribes to deceive the greedy European colonizers. Recent research also analyses the possibility that the mythology was created by the Spanish with the intention of concealing the constant massacres carried out in the continent's forest areas.

MYSTERIOUS DEATHS

In the first moments after the discovery of the New World, Europeans explored the myths created by the lost cities. A series of speculations confused the members of the expeditions indicating the location of "El Dorado" in different regions. Some Spaniards came to believe that the golden territory could be found in the Sonoran Desert in Mexico. Other beliefs pointed to "El Dorado" hidden at the source of the Amazon River. Groups of Europeans headed for Central America, carrying out expeditions in areas that had hitherto been unknown. The last place researched was the Guiana Plateau, located between Venezuela, Guyana, and the north of Brazil, in the state of Roraima. Over the centuries, the mystery has become the target of the curious. Some researchers never returned from their missions and mysteriously disappeared. It is speculated that they died in accidents in hostile parts of the jungle or as a result of animal attacks. Despite never having found any references to the legend, explorers have extracted a lot of gold and silver from Brazilian territory.

OTHER LEGENDS

The greed of Europeans in search of precious metals formed a long list of mythological stories related to lost civilizations. The legend of Paititi describes a hidden territory in the eastern Andes, situated somewhere in the rainforests of Peru, reaching as far north as Bolivia and southwest Brazil. In order to intimidate the Spanish colonizers, the Indians of the region said that the city belonged to an enchanted kingdom in the middle of the jungle, previously inhabited by a race of sun-worshipping creatures, the Ewaipanoma. All of them had no necks and their heads were located at chest level. Mythology disseminated the existence of palaces covered in gold. The supreme leader of the civilization was a man called "El Dorado" or the Golden Prince.

Still in the Amazon rainforest, the legend of Akakor presents a more recent version of the region's mystical cities. Its possible existence was only discovered in 1976 by German journalist Karl Brugger, during a visit to the Brazilian jungle. According to local Indian accounts, 15,000 years ago an ancient civilization hid riches in its stone constructions between the Amazon and Peru. The book "The Chronicles of Akakor", published by the journalist, brought several adventurers to the site in search of the lost society. Three researchers disappeared during the search and Brugger was murdered in Rio de Janeiro in 1984. It is speculated that the legend was created by the natives based on the stories of "El Dorado."

CURRENT TOURISM

The lost cities in Amazonas and Pará are now home to a native population that continues to preserve their stories and legends. In the region of Santarém, where the Tapajós Indians lived, tourists can visit the João Fona Cultural Centre. The site, which underwent an extensive revitalization process in 2015, has 12 rooms bringing together much of the city's history. Among the archaeological pieces from ancient civilization are ceramic artifacts, fossilized fish, examples of agricultural materials and newspapers with detailed records about the indigenous people. In the Marajó Museum, located on the island of the same name, travellers will find all aspects of the routine of the extinct population. Miniature boats used on the farms, the typical costumes of the tribes, re-imaginings of plantations, photos, everyday objects, and spears used in battles are among the items on display. Several inns in the city sell tours to tourists, including the museums and the archaeological sites.

Aerial view of the Amazon River from Belém do Pará

CONTROVERSIAL DISCOVERY OF THE CENTURY

10

LOST CITY OF THE MONKEY GOD: IN THE MIDDLE OF THE HONDURAS JUNGLE, THE DISCOVERY OF THIS CIVILIZATION WAS CONSIDERED THE MOST IMPORTANT ARCHAEOLOGICAL REVELATION OF OUR TIME

The mystical White City, also known as the Lost City of the Monkey God, is one of archaeology's most recent discoveries. There have always been many legends surrounding the ancient stories of this civilization, but the first traces left by its inhabitants were only found in mid-2013. Located in the Honduran forest, in the unexplored jungle of the Plátano River, the area has since received several expeditions led by scholars to gather more information about the lost community. So far, they have found evidence of an advanced metropolis, with ruins of plazas, pyramids, embankments, and artistic artifacts that have yet to be culturally explained. Although little information has been found about the ethnicity of the population, the country's authorities claim that they are not related to the Mayans, Aztecs, or Incas. Satellite images taken in the territory indicate the possibility of other ancient constructions hidden by the forest. It is believed that stone structures left over from palaces, houses and churches may soon be found.

INHOSPITABLE TERRITORY

Rumours about the White City have aroused the curiosity of many adventurers over the years. Explorers encountered serious difficulties in completing their research in the face of the hostility of the rainforests and the lack of objectivity about what they were looking for. As the legends never indicated the possible locations of the ruins, all the groups entered the jungle without any direction. The civilization's activities may have begun around the year 1000 BC, and it was nicknamed the city of the Monkey God after an American archaeologist discovered that the natives called it that. The most important record of the region, before the recent discovery, was reported by Theodore Morde and published in the New York Times in 1940. The supposed evidence found of the lost culture has never been proven geographically. In 1928, writer Charles Lindbergh also spotted ancient artifacts amid white ruins while flying over the Honduran forests. The reports helped spread the legend, increasing the number of expeditions to the site.

MODERN TECHNOLOGIES

Advances in research have only been possible with the use of electronic devices that identify inhospitable parts of the earth virtually. The function of the radar, called LIDAR, short for Light Detection and Ranging, is to reduce the time taken for excavations and expeditions by years. The technological device uses pulses of light to map a territorial extension by means of photos in 3D visualized models. All the work is done using lasers emitted from an airplane, flying over the jungle areas, and reaching the high elevations. Before the ruins were visualized, many scholars claimed that the forests of South and Central America were extremely hostile places for the growth of ancient civilizations. But discoveries made with the radar indicate the extinction of several prehistoric cities on the site, with still no concrete traces of their populations.

CURIOUS OBJECTS

Ground excavations carried out in 2015, in partnership with a team of experts from National Geographic, located 52 objects buried in the soil of the region. Among the curiosities recorded was a head with features similar to those of a jaguar. It is speculated that this is symbolic of the shaman rituals performed in the community.

Given its round shape, it is thought possible that the object was used as a kind of ball in games similar to today's soccer. In addition to the eccentric artifact, the teams also collected evidence of ingenious earthmoving techniques in the area. Faced with so much evidence, archaeologists are arguing that there were several advanced cities located in the territory in past times, forming a great empire.

Ruins in Honduras' forest region

PROTECTIVE MEASURES

The exact location of all the lost cities has been preserved by the investigative teams, at the request of the Honduran government. The security system was developed to protect the archaeological site from possible looters, as has happened in other areas of South and Central America. Some points in the region are used as routes for drug trafficking, worrying the authorities about the interest of gangs in the ancient material hidden in the jungle. The measures have generated a lot of controversy in Honduras and have been questioned by professionals involved in excavation processes. The famous archaeologist Ricardo Agurcia, a native of the country, refuted the findings of the White City. According to him, the team formed for the work was unreliable, due to the absence of Honduran specialists who knew the interests of the regional culture. Another argument raised by Agurcia was that it was strange that the news was first published by a US outlet.

FIRST ARTICLE

The first news about the discovery of the civilization was published in March 2015 on the National Geographic website. From then on, a series of discussions began about the veracity of the reports by the American team, led by Christopher Fisher. The territory, which was initially only seen by LIDAR resources, needed to be visited in person before being announced to the world as the main discovery of the century. The ground expedition included American and Honduran archaeologists, documentarians, ethnologists, anthropologists, engineers and 16 soldiers from the Honduran Special Security Forces. National Geographic sent a photographer and an editor to record the main moments of the excavation. In October 2015, the channel released the controversial documentary "Legend of the Monkey God", about the research process in the territory.

LIBYA'S ANCIENT HERITAGE

11

TRACES LEFT BY ANCIENT CIVILIZATIONS IN THE SAHARA TURN THE REGION INTO AN IMPRESSIVE ARCHAEOLOGICAL SITE FULL OF CULTURAL RICHES

Based on satellite and aerial photos, research teams from the University of Leicester in England found traces of a lost civilization in southwestern Libya, near the Sahara Desert, in 2011. The architectural techniques used in the construction of temples and castles impressed the scholars with their modern structures. Originally built with mud bricks mixed with clay, the ruins of the site are more than four meters high and were considered great civil works of the past. Despite the degradation caused by the passage of time, the entire structure of the archaeological site is very well preserved. The processes of soil exploitation created an effective irrigation system in the region, and some monuments are similar to the medieval palaces of the European monarchy. To date, more than 100 villages and rural work areas have been studied. It is speculated that the city existed between the years 100 and 500 of the Christian era.

ORGANIZED STATE

The archaeological research, led by academic David Mattingly, has received incentives of US$4 million from the European Union to try to identify elements that explain the cultural and social concept of this civilization. The population growth in the country's desert intrigues scientists. The region is considered one of the most hostile places in the world, reaching temperatures of up to 122 degrees Fahrenheit during the day. The discoveries made in the territory show that the society had a functional model of an organized state with a well-structured hierarchical system. Its inhabitants were very successful traders between neighbouring peoples, creating different solutions to survive the climatic conditions of the Libyan desert. In order to speed up trading, they developed various routes through the region, which still function today. Much of the evidence found indicates that the improvements were achieved by locating oases in the middle of the desert.

CIVIL WAR

The British team spent five years on the site, taking part in excavations and territorial surveys before the recent discovery. The archaeological work is concentrated around the town of German, formerly known as Garaman. In February 2011, Libya went through an extensive armed conflict led by rebels calling for the removal of dictator Muamar Gaddafi from power. Faced with an escalating civil war, David Mattingly had to leave the country and the search was called off. Eight months later, the former head of state was killed in an exchange of fire, ending a government that had overseen the Libyan people for more than four decades. Although the first traces of the ruins of Garamantes were found more than 30 years ago, intolerant political rule prevented further study of the region.

GARAMANTES PEOPLE

The entire structure of the unknown city was submerged among the ruins of the Kingdom of Garamantes. The pre-Islamic population of the territory was responsible for the construction of the monuments found, forming a veritable empire in their society. All the administrative power was in the capital of Germa, now the district of Jarma in Libya. Its first activities took place in the middle of the 5th century BC, the same time as the rise of the Roman Empire in Europe. It is believed that the political leaders expanded the community's domains to the Fezzan region, in the southwest of the country. Over the centuries, the Garamantes have been historically portrayed as barbaric men, nomads with no concept of civilization who moved chaotically between various areas of the desert. After the intensification of studies led by the British, a culture was discovered that was sophisticated and advanced in governmental aspects.

AFRICAN DOMINATION

Agricultural techniques ensured the distribution of food among the kingdom's inhabitants. Cultivation revolved around grapes, wheat, barley, and olives to produce substances like olive oil. There are indications that they discovered the compositions needed to work with salt refinement and glass materials. Rapid economic growth was achieved by exploiting slaves on the plantations, doubling the number of items traded. Researchers claim that this civilization acted as one of the most powerful empires in North Africa, leaving cultural legacies in various spheres of contemporary society. In addition to their sophisticated administrative system, the Garamantes also developed their own language, with writing methods used in various parts of the continent.

TROPICAL RAINS

By devising creative solutions to deal with the region's climatic issues, the Garamantes achieved a quality of life far superior to all the other peoples who inhabited the Libyan desert. The cities were planned, full of fruit trees, extending over a geographical area larger than that of Great Britain. The kingdom was active for over a thousand years, taking refuge in the valleys in times of drought. Even though temperatures rose much higher than expected, the territory often received tropical rains. A kind of green trail formed between the soil of sub--Saharan Africa and the Mediterranean coast, which attracted countless animals to the region.

FUNERARY ART

Initially, the members of the civilization built their dwellings inside caves located around the desert. After developing water procedures, in the year 1000 BC, they adapted temples as dwellings for the population. At the time, there were from 50 to 100 thousand people living in the society. One of the ingenious solutions to the lack of water in times of drought was to excavate the ground, forming approximately 600 tunnels that resulted in 100,000 wells 131.24 feet deep. The archaeological site of Garamantes preserves a kind of cemetery occupied by 100 tombs. Intended for the rulers of the ancient city, the site was built using bricks mixed with large quantities of clay. The bodies of ordinary people received a less special fate, being sent to plots of land around the nearby valleys. Little is known about whether there was any religious ritual during the burial of politically important figures.

HISTORICAL HERITAGE

For researchers, the image preserved for centuries of the Garamante people as nomadic and violent men is related to the Roman Empire's efforts to try to halt the kingdom's rapid economic growth. Until then, the civilization was treated with contempt by the academic and scientific world for its supposed lack of contribution to ethnological studies. Representatives sent by the Romans arrived in the Libyan desert around 19 BC with the mission of conquering the territory. For the empire's leaders, the measure prevented any attempt to attack European expeditions in the African desert. Under the command of Lucius Cornelius Balbo, the Romans would have lost several commercial actions due to the expansion of the Garamantes' activities. The great aim of the excavations carried out by the British team is to put the true history of this lost civilization into school books and into the cultural memory of Libyans.

POPULATION EXTINCTION

The kingdom built by the Garamantes collapsed in the face of the climatic conditions imposed on North Africa. Although they had created solutions considered advanced for the long dry seasons in the region, the population succumbed to the scarcity of water in the desert. During the 4th century, after resisting the limits imposed by the lack of water resources for 600 years, a large part of the civilization became extinct, with its members dying of thirst and hunger. The entire political concentration of power was divided between small city-states that were formed to house the remaining people. Before long, Islamic tribes dominated the territory, leaving the traces of Garamante society covered up by the sands of the region. Until 2011, the little that was known about them was taken from writings left by the Roman Empire.

AFRICAN COLONIZATION

From 146 BC, Rome began the process of dominating African civilizations. Representatives of the empire settled in regions close to the Mediterranean Sea. The territory underwent several other invasions by peoples interested in forming new colonies to plunder its natural wealth, such as the Greeks, Arabs, French, Portuguese, English and Spanish. To this day, the marks left by Greco-Roman antiquity on Libya's coastal towns can be seen in the form of ruins that are constantly visited by tourists. Among all the cultures imposed during the invasions, the influence left by the Arabs predominates in the lifestyle adopted by the country. In the capital, Tripoli, preserved buildings recall details of Libya's past, highlighting the Roman Empire and the Phoenician civilization. The main pieces found by archaeologists are in the Jamahiriya Museum. Another popular spot is the lost city of Sabratha, west of Tripoli. Among the historic ruins are huge Roman temples.

Roman archaeological site in Tripoli, capital of Libya

THE CULTURAL LEGACY OF MINOAN SOCIETY

12

DESTROYED BY A SEQUENCE OF NATURAL DISASTERS, THE CIVILIZATION INSPIRED VARIOUS CONCEPTS ADOPTED BY THE GREEKS OVER THE CENTURIES

LOST CIVILIZATIONS

Minoan paintings depicting animals in the daily life of civilization

In the mid-2000s BC, the inhabitants of the island of Crete in Greece built a society that was considered extremely modern by the standards of the time. One of the factors that helped their rapid growth was the fertility of the soil in the region south of the Aegean Sea. Little is known about the inner workings of this civilization, since experts have never managed to decipher its elaborate forms of writing. With a deep knowledge of the region's seas, the Minoans organized the country's first great naval power. They transported a variety of products, most of which were made by the people themselves, such as gold artifacts, fabrics, olive oil and grapes.

The historical ruins left by the community are gathered in the city of Knossos, the main commercial and cultural centre of the past. The archaeological site dates to the main customs of the first people to occupy Greek lands. The truth about the origin of these people has not yet been found, but it is known that it all began with the arrival of Neolithic groups in the region. Peaceful, they became known for the bureaucratic way they settled their political affairs and for their respect for women.

EVOLVED ARCHITECTURE

With an ingenious architectural vision, the Minoans built huge palaces, based on concepts considered advanced for the time. The most famous monument is the Palace of Knossos, with five floors and around 1,300 rooms. The entire space was divided between various functions, serving as accommodation for nobles from other regions, workshops for ceramic artists and religious rooms. The walls had decorative items like today's luxurious hotels, including paintings symbolizing the city's routine. The numerous palaces built on the island are the ruins with the best internal finish ever found by archaeologists and researchers. Remaining documents show that the ancient buildings have unique characteristics, designed especially to meet the needs of the nobles. The basis of the region's architecture was brick, clay, and stone. The spaces, full of complex corridors, had colourful drawings of wild animals in the main rooms.

AGRICULTURE

The groups settled on the island grew wheat and lentils and sold luxury goods to merchants from Egypt and other nearby regions. They fed themselves by fishing, which was facilitated by the mild climate prevailing in the Greek Sea. They developed small farms, raising oxen, sheep, and goats, far from the commercial movement of the big cities. On some occasions, the animals were used to supplement the meals of local families. With commercial success on the rise, Minoan society colonized a series of geographical extensions around Crete over the years. Schemes of sale and exchange were carried out by means of weights and

Internal ruins of the Minoan palace in Crete

measures of products, valuing the food items generated in abundance in the territory. During the period known as the Bronze Age, between 3000 BC and 1200 BC, the inhabitants of the community discovered the uses of copper to replace stone in various functions. They built vessels, harbours for their large fleet of ships and advanced furnace systems.

ANCIENT CITIES

During the period of social and commercial growth, some parts of the island functioned as a metropolis. All the cities were connected to each other by roads designed to facilitate the production system and labour negotiations. They also built a modern sewage system made up of stone ducts that carried away rainwater. Stores full of decorative items and foodstuffs bustled in the commercial centres, surrounded by houses and buildings. The main streets were paved, distributing houses in blocks, much like condominiums. In areas further away from the centre, peasants lived in villages built from wood and bricks based on limestone masses. In some communities, the inhabitants built large mansions in the middle of agricultural areas. On the edges of the coast, the Minoans founded factories specializing in the production of their ships, and some districts were home to a large concentration of artisan workshops.

ARTISTIC ELEMENTS

Many characteristics of Minoan society have been discovered through the traces left by their ceramic work. They produced large-scale clay and eggshell vessels for storing wine, oil, and wheat. Artistic techniques were also widely used in palace decorations. The daily life of civilization was often recorded in symmetrical features identified as animals, plants, and human features. In the Greek past, the bull was considered a sacred figure and was depicted on various items sold in the island's cities. Places inhabited by nobles were painted with decorative ceramics on the walls. The artists created richly detailed scenes of festivals full of distinguished guests, local ceremonies, and marriage celebrations. Before they were finished, the ceramic pieces were fired in kilns to solidify their shapes. One of the main styles used by the Minoans became known as Pyrgos. The method, formed by smoky designs with polished, linear shapes, refers to the Greek city of the same name, also dominated by the civilization.

FEMALE FIGURE

The religiosity adopted by the members of Minoan society mixed their hierarchical ceremonies with moments of worshipping the gods. For the Greek leaders, spiritual beings were directly linked to the forces of nature, which led to the habit of making various offerings around the Aegean Sea. There is practically no archaeological evidence to prove the religious beliefs followed by the city's inhabitants, but repeated sculptures found throughout the territory indicate the existence of a mother goddess, seen by the Greeks as a sovereign deity. Various works of art, including paintings and statues, show women wearing make-up and sensual corsets that reveal part of their breasts. Most scholars believe that the Minoans considered the female figure to be a symbol of fertility, especially the intimate parts of her body. Members of Crete's nobility took part in many parties held in palaces, always with wine and traditional local delicacies. The gatherings were carefully organized by the influential women of the colonized Greek cities. Although they did not have the same administrative functions as the noblemen, the lady monarchs earned great respect from their subjects.

MYTHOLOGICAL HISTORY

The British researcher Arthur Evans was the first to find archaeological remains left by the ancient Greeks in the 19th century. As there are no records of the true name of the civilization active on the island of Crete, he named it the Minoan society in allusion to the cultural mythology of King Minos. According to legend, the Labyrinth of Crete, built by the craftsman Daedalus, was a monument designed especially for the Minotaur. The character, half human, half bull, was extremely popular among the people due to the strong symbolism of the animal in the community. The theory is believed to have originated in the architecture of the Palace of Knossos. The poorest citizens only saw the monument from the outside, hearing stories of its resemblance to a labyrinth. The ruins of the building are, to this day, one of the most visited tourist attractions in Greece and contain many mythological tales linked to the existence of King Minos, considered to be the son of Zeus.

DEVASTATING EARTHQUAKE

In 1700 BC, a violent earthquake destroyed the island of Crete and its main monuments, such as the palaces of Knossos, Malia, Kato and Zakros. After a short period, the region was completely rebuilt, housing even more people. Throughout the process of renovating the palaces, various groups specializing in civil works supervised the work. New sewage systems were installed and a season of statues representing the city's routine developed, constantly exalting the female figure. At the same time, men dedicated to maritime duties-built ships capable of crossing the entire length of the Mediterranean Sea. The golden phase of civilization took place during the early Neo-Palatial period. The Minoan domains spread to other colonies in the Aegean Sea and Sicily. Trade routes reached more and more territories, supplying the Greek economy, and transforming cities into veritable empires.

After a long period of consecutive success, Crete's culture began to decline at the end of the 15th century BC. A new earthquake, now of greater proportions, hit the island, destroying all the commercial centres and its main monuments, including the Palace of Knossos. The eruption of a volcano on the island of Santorini brought an intense tsunami that wiped out all the ports used by the city's navy. The damaged soil created serious difficulties for food production. Pressured by economic and social problems, the Minoans waged an extensive civil war between the colonies. The chaotic climate in the region facilitated the invasion of Dorian groups from the mountainous expanses of Greece. In the middle of 1380 BC, the last inhabitants of the civilization of Crete fled to the east of the country.

CULTURAL LEGACY

The cultural advances made by Minoan society influenced various peoples who later inhabited the regions around the Aegean Sea. The legacy left by the people of Crete represents the ideals of a peaceful, religious, and respectful people in relation to the position of women in cultural, social, and administrative aspects. One of the most sophisticated societies in Greek culture was directly inspired by the concepts promoted by the Minoans. The Mycenaean civilization rose with great artistic talent, adopting equal rights for local women. It existed between 1600 BC and 1050 BC. Little is known about the reasons that led to its disappearance, but some historians are betting on a new attack by the Dorians on the territory.

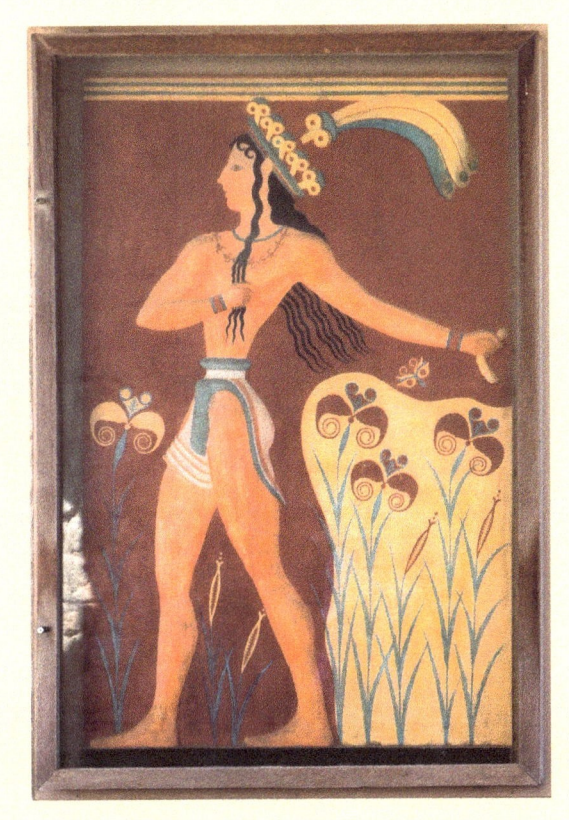

Minoan painting depicting the clothes worn by men

THE CLOTHES WORN BY THE MINOANS

Women played an important social role in civilization. Their clothes were considered modern for the time, with lots of ruffles, a shaped waist, and adjustments in the breast area. All the garments were cut to fit the curves of the female body. The elongated fabric formed elegant dresses that were often accompanied by hat-like accessories. They combed their hair carefully and always appeared clean and well groomed.

Men wore a kind of male loincloth that could be made of wool, leather, or linen, depending on the temperature of each occasion. The structure of the garment highlighted the waist, giving the garment the appearance of a smaller figure. It is speculated that this may be a sign that the Minoans had been wearing the same loincloth since they were teenagers. On the other hand, the nobles of the community were very fond of wearing jewellery in public appearances, such as amethyst stones, agate pearls and rock crystal.

THE MYSTICAL KINGDOM OF ATLANTIS

13

THE PERFECT CITY DESCRIBED BY PLATO IS ONE OF THE GREATEST UNKNOWNS OF WORLD, WHICH CONTINUES ITS SEARCH WITH THE INTENTION OF FINDING IT AT THE BOTTOM OF THE OCEAN

Although it is not officially considered an ancient civilization, the story of Atlantis represents one of the greatest myths of humanity at different times. According to the best-known version of the legend, the lost city disappeared meteorically in just over a day and a night.

The centre of golden and beautiful lands formed a powerful and extremely populous empire. The entire social and cultural structure had been built in front of the Mediterranean Sea, on an island left over from the Atlantic continent. The inhabitants were divided between agricultural activities, used for their own food and trade, handicrafts, and the security services of the local military guard. In the religious field, they fervently worshipped the ancient gods popular in Greek culture. Animals were domesticated and often used as a way of demonstrating sovereignty among the nobility. In the centre of the city, legendarily described as rectangular, there were a multitude of orchards with abundant productions of different fruits every season. These harmonious features are mainly responsible for Atlantis constantly being compared to the biblical paradise.

PHILOSOPHICAL QUOTES

The first reference to Atlantis was made by the Greek philosopher Plato in two of his major works during the 4th century BC. In the first essay, the narrative uses the statements of the main character to report the existence of a community located beyond the Columns of Hercules, in the Strait of Gibraltar. In "Critias" or "Atlantis", the philosopher clarifies various internal characteristics of the mysterious city, beginning the first legends about the Atlantean people. Plato tells of the wonders of the culture established in the society, detailing the religiosity, the natural beauty of the region and the architecture of the temples, with monuments covered in gold. Faced with the philosopher's vision of Atlantis, even the most skeptic Greeks came to believe that it was a perfect civilization, driven by extremely just laws. Some theories related to the myth of the lost city believe that Plato may have written his accounts based on the existence of an emerging community on the island of Thera more than 3,500 years ago. A small group of scientists, on the other hand, argue that the whole thing is just a creative fable invented by the philosopher to enhance popular imagination.

POSEIDON KINGDOM

According to the stories told by Plato, the gods of Greek mythology divided themselves up to take care of all the sources of nature, becoming sovereigns in their specialty. The empire where the society of Atlantis lived was ruled by Poseidon, the God of the Seas. After millennia of solitude, he fell in love with a young human girl called

Cleitó. Concerned for the safety of his beloved, who lived on a mountain in the centre of the city, the ruler decided to isolate the territory, enclosing all the spaces with water, earth, walls, and moats. From this unusual union, five sets of twin sons were born. As a way of remaining recognized for his unwavering sense of justice, the deity divided the island's geographical extent into ten parts, giving each descendant a piece of land. The eldest heir was baptized Atlas and from his earliest years underwent intense training to receive power after his father left the throne. Atlas would later become the mythological giant who held up the heavens. For centuries, in Greek tradition, the first-born son of each of the kings took his place in succession. Despite being guided by ideals of equality, the gods ruled with an iron fist and could condemn offenders to merciless deaths.

SOVEREIGN RITUALS

There was a kind of jury court formed by the monarchs, which met every four or five years to discuss the administrative issues of Greece and judge the decisions taken internally by each one. All measures needed Poseidon's approval before they could be put into practice. During the event, traditional Atlantean rites took place, in which the kings were surrounded by several bulls in a courtyard at the Temple of Poseidon. The main point of the ceremony consisted of the moment when the animals were beheaded and had their blood spread over the bodies of the gods. At the end, the remains of the bulls were burned in

Statue of Atlas, the giant who held up the heavens

a bonfire, while each ruler pronounced an extensive oath of loyalty and respect to the Greek territories. Although the legends do not reveal the exact number of inhabitants of Atlantis, Plato described the island's territorial extension as larger than Libya and Asia combined. According to scholars, the Greeks did not know the exact geographical size of these places at the time.

POPULAR MYTHOLOGY

According to Plato, Atlantis had disappeared 9,000 years before he existed. The absence of physical records of the civilization was caused by the destruction carried out by colonizers from all continents. Most invaders, upon gaining power, ordered the burning of any material related to the stories of each people's past. The myth of Atlantis is so popular that over 5,000 books, articles and magazines about the lost city have been published around the world over the centuries. Another aspect of the legendary story of the lost island defines the territory as the first civilization on the planet. Until then, all men were considered barbarians.

The government formed by the Greek gods achieved so much power that the society's domains expanded to the Mississippi River, the Gulf of Mexico, the west coast of Europe and Africa, the Black Sea, the Caspian Sea, and the Pacific coast of South America. All these places would have been populated by descendants of the Atlanteans, ensuring the formation of civilizations as well-structured as the one that existed in ancient Greece. It is speculated that the first area colonized by Atlantis was Egypt, in a social reproduction exactly similar to the way of life

Statue of Poseidon, God of the Seas, at the bottom of the sea in Greece

adopted on the island. Scientifically, there is no evidence to prove that Atlantean explorers passed through these places. In Plato's tales, the inhabitants of Athens even duelled the Atlantean army to prevent the confiscation of their land.

WRATH OF THE GODS

It was precisely this desire to conquer other territories that was largely responsible for the disappearance of the civilization. As the gods provided everything the inhabitants needed on the island, it was believed that they lived happily in their own private paradise. However, the colonization of other regions demonstrated the concentration of selfish feelings among the population. The wealth and power that existed on Atlantis were no longer enough for its inhabitants, who craved more and more precious material artifacts. Known for its harmonious villages, the lost island became a hostile environment, with various fights between the leaders of the expeditions, who at that time were trying to dominate the capital, Athens.

The ambition of the people grew to enormous proportions and the conflicts escalated to the point where Zeus, the god of Olympus, called an extraordinary assembly of all the deities of mythology to decide what punishment would be meted out to the population. The most talked about hypothesis is that Atlantis was punished with aquatic earthquakes that invaded its entire territorial extension, dragging the entire island to the bottom of the sea without leaving any trace of its existence.

ATLANTEAN WRITING

In some mythologies, the inhabitants of the island communicated through the Basque language. The language is one of the most isolated in the world today, being used only by the Basque country itself, located between northeastern Spain and southwestern France. The dialects are so rare that they are not classified in the official groups of European languages. The word-forming elements bear a little resemblance to the expressions used by the Inca peoples and the Ural-Altaic societies, made up of Finns, Hungarians, Turks, and Estonians. The composition of large sentences spoken in just one word is also reminiscent of the languages used by Eskimos and indigenous tribes. The writing system related to the creation of the symbolic language alphabet would have been used by the Atlanteans to describe everyday events in manuscripts. The name of the island itself may have been very different from Atlantis, which was probably developed by Plato in his works.

SOUTH AMERICAN RELATIONSHIP

Although most assumptions locate the lost island of Atlantis in regions of the Atlantic Ocean, renowned Peruvian physicist Enrico Mattievich has decided to question this thesis. He argues that the ancient civilization was a settlement in South America. Studies into this hypothesis began 35 years ago, after the physicist visited the Chavin de Huantar Palace in his homeland. Filled with archaeological remains, the site displayed the figure of Medusa reflected in a rock. The character is described in Greek mythology as the female image of a monster with snake-like hair. The cultural symbolism contained in the engraving inspired the physicist to research in detail a possible link between the South American continent and Greece. In addition to the rock of Medusa, several artifacts found in the palace also caught Mattievich's attention.

Based on his studies, he identified a kind of gold and silver alloy that turned reddish when it encountered copper. The metal, called coriculque, was developed by the Inca Empire and would be very similar to oricalto, theoretically believed to be popular in Atlantis. For the physicist, the Atlanteans discovered most of South America in order to exploit the region's natural riches. The statements in Plato's narratives would have erroneously added up the dates of activities in Atlantis due to the lack of historical documents to prove the legends.

ARISTOTLE'S VERSION

The best known of Plato's pupils, the Greek philosopher Aristotle, considered the way the story of Atlantis was finished to be completely unrealistic. When he concluded his studies, he set up a school very similar to that of his master, becoming a direct competitor. Among his most famous apprentices was Alexander the Great, one of the famous kings of ancient Greece. For Aristotle, the city of Atlantis never existed. The whole myth would have been created in Plato's mind to please the public with an intense mystery narrative. Over the centuries, many experts have shown the same skepticism towards the mythology of Atlantis. Much of the academic world approaches the subject with a certain disregard, believing it to be just a popular fable. However, there are several groups of researchers who claim that it is impossible to ignore the island's existence in the past. For them, historians dismiss the evidence simply out of fear that they have made grotesque mistakes by mocking Plato's writings. Teams enthusiastic about the technological advances available today intend to use the resources to carry out new research and more detailed excavations on the subject.

RECORDED REMAINS

From time to time, news comes out about the discovery of ruins believed to be from Atlantis. In 1986 alone, the civilization was "rediscovered" twice. The first report came from geographical areas near the Mediterranean Sea. The second report came from the Bahamas, in areas linked to the district of Bimini. In the region northwest of the capital, Nassau, a temple of Atlantis is said to be slowly returning to the surface. Two Cayce Foundation pilots claim to have photographed the ruins during flights near the district. The team was precisely looking for visual proof of the reports in the press. Marine excavations concluded that the submerged monument has stones in its foundations and the walls are preserved.

However, no connection with the lost city has been confirmed. As the building is very close to the port, security measures had to be taken at the time to prevent the actions of treasure looters. Over the years, various pieces of evidence have appeared relating to Greek mythology. One of the most interesting was found around the Caribbean islands. At the bottom of the ocean, off the coast of Haiti, there was an entire submerged city. Although they have not solved the great mystery, the remains have surprised archaeologists by proving that these regions were once made up of dry land. With each discovery of ruins, new theories about Atlantis emerge. In 2015, Spaniard Manuel Cuevas, a specialist in Greek mythology, claimed to have located the lost city in the deep waters of the Doñana National Park, in the Andalusia region of Spain. According to images captured by virtual satellites, he claims that the ruins are the same as Plato's quotes depicting the area as circular, about 4.96 miles long.

STORIES AND LEGENDS OF LEMURIA

14

BETWEEN MYTHOLOGIES DEBATED FOR CENTURIES AND TIRELESS RESEARCH, THE UNKNOWN TERRITORY AROUSES THE INTEREST OF SCHOLARS FROM VARIOUS SCIENTIFIC BACKGROUNDS

Illustration of men in the Ice Ages, when the planet's temperature dropped sharply

Surrounded by legends and mysteries, the history of the continent of Mu, also known as Lemuria, remains without archaeological evidence to this day. According to the best-known theories, the expanse of land was submerged somewhere in the Pacific Ocean. Discussions on the subject began in the 19th century and, over the years, have brought together the opinions of various experts from all over the world. Very popular among followers of the occult, catastrophic thinking argues that major natural tragedies are the main causes of geographical and ethnic changes on Earth. Created by the naturalist Georges Cuvier in 1812, the revolutionary philosophy was also adopted in the Tamil Nadu region of India and is considered one of the possible explanations for this mystery. Metaphysical groups took part in research in search of evidence left behind by the peoples who would have inhabited Mu. Although they contributed to the spread of other myths about the lost continent, they failed to record any important discoveries. Some ethnologists relate the particularities of Lemuria to the cultural routine of the people of Atlantis. Even though they lived together for a short time, when the civilization mentioned by Plato disappeared, the inhabitants of Mu were just beginning their first activities.

CONTROVERSIAL INFORMATION

The exact location of Lemuria is one of the most controversial topics for geographers. According to the most widely accepted version, the continent was submerged in the region called the "Ring of Fire". The elevated, highly unstable area lies to the west of the Americas, to the east of Asia and Oceania. Natural phenomena cause earthquakes and other devastating tragedies on different scales in the region. It is speculated that after long periods of inactivity, the land area belonging to this zone could convulse again, causing major territorial and geological changes of long duration, as happened during the glacial period.

Before disappearing as a result of the violent eruption of a volcano, the inhabitants of Mu may have received countless signals from nature indicating the proximity of a catastrophe. Even though they lived in a very advanced society for the time, the people were unaware of the possibility of such severe territorial changes. One of the few unanimities among scholars is about the period of existence of the lost continent, supposedly during prehistoric times.

THIRD RACE

There are several divergent stories about the lives of the inhabitants of Mu. Most accounts indicate that the civilization achieved metropolitan status, developing social and technological advances. Legends linked to the occult, on the other hand, claim that the men of Lemuria dedicated themselves to studying and practicing black magic. A third hypothesis has further increased curiosity about the origin of these peoples. According to scholars of Theosophy, the inhabitants of the submerged continent belonged to a third race - beings over 16 feet tall, considered human with the characteristics of reptiles and dragons. The reptilian hypothesis was created by the influential Russian writer Madame Blavatsky, the main leader of the Theosophical Society. At different times, people from Cambodia, India and Australia spread this claim about Lemuria while researching the subject. The continent's natives were also said to be three-eyed hermaphrodites, with the third located at the back of the head. For theosophists, humanity has experienced four stages of evolution. The human structure of the inhabitants of Mu would be the first associated with a physical body.

SOCIAL THEORIES

In its heyday, Mu may have been a fertile continent, full of gold, copper, and silver. There were many legends about the population of Lemuria before Europeans arrived in America. After the discovery of the New Continent in 1492, the myths were considered irrelevant for a long time as much of the culture of the colonized territories died out. The occult writer James Churchward was one of the first to revive the discussion on the subject by deciphering various traces written on stones. In 1926, he published the literary work "The Lost Continent of Mu: Homeland of Man", in which he recounted details of his excavations and discoveries. The written records about the society defined its location

Illustration of the Garden of Eden, according to the description from the Bible

slightly below the equator. Other geographically important information revealed that the area stretched 5,952 miles from east to west, and 2,976 miles from north to south. The writer had access to all this data while on an extensive military mission in India. Several local priests were said to have contributed to the research by indicating, during the 1880s, suitable places to find traces of the continent. One of the priests even believed that he was one of the descendants of the Lemurian civilization.

THE GARDEN OF EDEN

Scientifically, most of the information written by Churchward is just legend spread by the Indians. However, his stories have become famous and have contributed to the awakening of many specialists interested in studying the region. One of the best-known myths claims that the expanse of the continent is the Garden of Eden, where human beings originated more than 200,000 years ago. According to biblical tradition, specifically in the Book of Genesis, God created Adam and Eve to cultivate and prosper this sacred ground. The territory would have undergone consecutive changes until it was inhabited by the community of Mu. Based on this assumption, various other speculations have arisen, guaranteeing that all the world's inhabitants are descendants of the peoples of the lost continent. The settlers of the region would have separated due to racial differences and migrated to build other legendary civilizations, such as Atlantis and the Uyghur empire. The revelation linked to the sacred scriptures led fanatical religious groups to take an interest in studying the mysteries of Mu.

> Currently, a group of Americans claim to be descendants of the inhabitants of Mu. According to their theories, some members of the prehistoric population managed to escape and prospered in other territories. Only a few people from this clan were chosen to receive spiritual guidance from their ancestors.

ADVANCED SOCIETY

The greatest achievements of the inhabitants of Mu were the construction of megalithic monuments, which were extremely advanced for the period of their existence. Each building was ingeniously designed to withstand a series of natural disasters. Various theories show that this system failed, as the civilization disappeared as a result of earthquakes and major upheavals in the "Ring of Fire" region. Divided into hierarchical systems, the prehistoric community would have adopted a simplified concept of monarchist government, responsible for the dissemination of local languages and scriptures. It is speculated that each inhabitant could only be considered an adult when they reached the age of 28. Studies on universal issues were compulsory for much of a native's life. According to versions that have yet to be verified by archaeologists, the people's domain extended between Hawaii, Easter Island and Fiji, in Oceania. Despite the lack of credibility of some of the theories put forward, many scientists claim that there really are several reasons why all parts of the same continent disappeared into the ocean.

NATIVE MONKEYS

Charles Darwin, author of the theory of evolution, mentioned the existence of Lemuria when trying to explain the geography of animal and plant species. According to the information gathered by the famous naturalist, the territory was home to native monkeys that later spread to Madagascar, India, and some areas of southern Africa. In order to complete long-distance journeys at such advanced levels, Mu's primates would have needed to rely on a terrestrial expanse made up of interconnected strips between continental dimensions, which later disappeared. The lost zone also came to be known as Lemuria after British zoologist Philip Sclate chose this name to identify the continental strips highlighted by Darwin. In some theories, the lack of cultural evidence of society would have caused a hole in anthropology by preventing records of evolution in the interval between apes and humans.

BRAZILIAN ATLANTIS

In May 2013, expeditions carried out by the Geological Survey of Brazil, in partnership with the Japanese Agency for Science and Technology of the Earth and Sea (Jamstec) located evidence relevant to world archaeology. 930 miles off the southeast coast of Brazil there was a continent that may have sunk after severe tectonic plate movements. Since the discovery, scholars have been working to prove the disappearance of the giant plateau in the shallowest region of the Upper Rio Grande uplift. To collect material remaining in the ocean, the teams used the technology of a device called the Shinkai 6500. The Japanese device can reach a depth of 21,326.5 feet. During previous work with drainage, the Brazilian researchers had already found granite compositions linked to the continent on the ocean floor.

Some archaeologists believe that the material found may have come loose from the territory occupied today by the city of São Paulo. Diving activities lasted an average of eight hours, submerging to 13,780.2 feet. The experts collected continental rocks, but also found unknown marine species in a critical state of habitation and deep-water corals. The expedition was nicknamed Iatá-Piuna after Brazil. The name was taken from the Tupi-Guarani and means "sailing through deep, dark waters". In addition to the stretches of the Rio Grande Rise, the teams visited Cape Town in South Africa and the São Paulo mountain range.

MAYAN REMAINS

In 1864, French author Charles Étienne Brasseur de Bourbourg discovered archives in a library in Madrid, Spain, that had allegedly belonged to the Mayan peoples living in Central America. The notes contained translation keys for the symbols used in the extinct civilization's writing. In view of the discoveries made with the manuscript, researchers deciphered information about the history of Mu. The documents recounted the events of an ancient society that had been dominated by the forces of the ocean after suffering volcanic eruptions. Two images very similar to the letters M and U could be identified in the texts. The lines told the story of a dispute between two brothers for the hand of the territory's queen. The competition resulted in the death of one of them, opening the way to glory for the survivor. During the natural tragedies that wiped out the continent, the queen fled to an area protected by the goddess "Isis". According to legends, she was responsible for the creation of the Sphinx and Egyptian civilization.

THE CIMMERIAN WARRIORS' BLOODY LEGACY

15

EXPELLED FROM THEIR HOMELAND, THE CIMMERIAN POPULATION BECAME KNOWN AS NOMADIC WARRIORS WILLING TO DO ANYTHING IN SEARCH OF WEALTH

The Cimmerian people existed around 1300 BC, building their civilization in the North Caucasus region, located near one of the borders between Eastern Europe and Asia, around the Sea of Azov. The first historical mention of the population appeared in the annual records organized by the kingdom of Assyria in mid-714 BC. The account described how the troops of the ruler Sargon II were helped by a community, supposedly called the Ghimire, to defeat the empire of Uratu, centred on the plateau of Armenia. It is speculated that the homeland of the Cimmerians was a territory known as Gamir or Uishdish, located in the buffer state of Mannai. In archaeological definitions, information on the origin of the Cimmerians is extremely scarce. However, it is believed that they were Indo-European peoples. Shortly afterwards, the population was expelled from the Caucasus by the Scythians, groups of nomadic Iranian shepherds, and headed for Anatolia. Several speculations about this period indicate that the Cimmerians accepted mercenaries, known as Khumri, into their community. Most of the time, the entry of members was consented to by King Sargon II.

BLOODY DOMAINS

It is speculated that civilization groups plundered the Kingdom of Uratu, causing the wrath of Sargon II. During a long conflict, the Cimmerian warriors destroyed the ruler's army and then murdered him. The process of population migration was closely monitored by the Assyrians, who were possibly plotting revenge for the tragedy that had befallen their king. Around 696 BC, they occupied large parts of the territory of Phrygia, today's Turkey. The local monarchs were captured, tortured by the invaders, and executed days later. Only the legendary King Midas, a character from Greek mythology, resisted the nomadic warriors by ingesting poison and dying before he could be arrested. The heyday of the Cimmerian population is believed to have occurred in 652 BC, when they took over the region of Sardis, the capital of Lydia. All invasions followed the same process of spreading panic with their war troops, willing to shed blood in search of new lands. Under the command of a new leader, known as Teushpa, they attacked the area that had hitherto belonged to Tabal and Cilicia. However, the army assembled by King Esarhaddon of Assyria managed to defeat them before their ideals were realized. The battle is said to have taken place in parts of Hubushna, a place that some theories claim to be Cappadocia.

WAR STRATEGY

Dejected by their recent failure, the Cimmerians decided to take over other parts of the Kingdom of Lydia. Concerned about the constant actions of these invaders, nobles from various neighbouring regions decided to unite their armies in order to definitively overthrow their opponents' high battle power. The war partnership between the Lydians and Assyrians was

Mesopotamian sculpture depicting the kings of Babylon and ancient Assyria

founded on a treaty that guaranteed the payment of tributes by King Gyges through the aid provided by the additional troops. The Cimmerian population, however, only resumed their invasion strategies ten years later. They returned to the territory during the rise of the empire built by Gyges' heir, the ruler Ardis II. The Cimmerian warriors used the same bloody occupation strategies that continued to terrorize the inhabitants of the cities. They invaded the main commercial points of Sardis, leading a series of plundering actions that closed almost all the villages in the region. A great epidemic may have been one of the reasons why the occupation of the land by the Cimmerian population was less intense than on other occasions. Around 626 BC, they were defeated again by men commanded by Alyattes II. With the execution of a large part of the Cimmerian warrior troop, the Lydian peoples heard no other reports of attacks in their midst.

CULTURAL BELIEFS

According to historical records, the Cimmerian community is usually referred to as Iranians or, on some occasions, as Thracians, Indo-Europeans originally from the regions of Thrace in southwestern Europe. Faced with expulsion from what they thought was their homeland by the Scythians in the Caucasus, the noble representatives of the ancient city split into groups to fight for the right to be buried near the tombs of their ancestors. As not all the Cimmerian monarchs agreed on the strategic issues of this battle, they ended up fighting among themselves, resulting in many deaths. The common members of the civilization, such as peasants and merchants, were traditionally buried around the river Tyras. After the disappearance of the population in Lydia, the warriors are believed to have migrated to the lands of Cappadocia, where they remained anonymously. According to theories put forward by the Greek historian Herodotus, the Cimmerians and Thracians were close relatives, originally inhabiting the Black Sea coast.

NATIVE LANGUAGE

Greek accounts of the customs of these people indicate that the remaining tribes in other territories would have adopted the Catacombic culture, which was very popular in the south of ancient Russia. Some traces of the language developed by the Cimmerians have been found in manuscripts left by the Assyrians. Theories spread over the centuries claim that the language spoken by the Indo-Europeans was the link between the dialects used by Thracian and Iranian communities. Several kings of the civilization were mentioned in writings from Greece and the Mesopotamian Empire, among them Tugdamme and Sandakshatru, who was in power during the late 7th century BC. Most of the records about the Cimmerians were told by their enemies after their violent attacks. Several legends surrounding the occupation of the Caucasus claim that the Cimmerian people were divided into monarchs and commoners to face the arrival of the Scythians. The nobility chose to resist and fight to the death. The population, on the other hand, decided to migrate towards Lydia, located to the east of ancient Ionia. According to the writings of Herodotus, the tombs of the dead aristocrats can still be seen in the lost territory.

MYTHOLOGICAL QUOTES

Over the centuries, the legends associated with the Cimmerians have been mentioned in various writings of other peoples. One of the most talked about quotes came from the records produced by the Assyrians. Theoretically, the lineage of the Franks, led by the Merovingian kings, emerged from predecessor tribes called the Sicambri. However, mythological stories very popular among these people claimed that their true ancestors were groups of Cimmerians sheltered in the region. Some historians have investigated the possibility that the ancestors of the Celtic and Germanic peoples had hereditary links with the Indo-Europeans. Although they used the exacerbated similarity between the terms of the ancient communities as their main argument, the claims were discredited by the impossibility of these populations having been in Western Europe during the 7th century BC. Subsequently, it has been speculated

Mesopotamian sculpture depicting Assyrians

that remnant groups of Cimmerian warriors may have moved to Nordic countries and stretches of the river Rhine. One of the indications that could prove this myth would be the tribe of Cimbri, founded in northern Denmark.

SCYTHIAN MYSTERIES

The population of the Scythians, responsible for colonizing the Caucasus after the expulsion of the Cimmerians, transformed the region into an important village. The nomadic tribe continued to plunder other areas, taking advantage of their equestrian skills. They were one of the first communities to use horses as a means of transportation during classical antiquity. The animal was also part of the diet of the population, who ate its meat and drank milk from the mares. When a member of the Scythian troops died during a mission, his animal was sacrificed and given a respectful burial in areas considered noble in the cities.

The Greek historian Herodotus was also directly interested in the cultural and social history of these people. According to his studies, the Scythians took part in some mysterious ceremonies in which they used the skulls of their dead opponents as drinking cups and consumed marijuana. Violence was one of the main characteristics of their invasions, as they always attacked their opponents with iron swords, arrows, spears and barbs capable of piercing various parts of the body. In search of hidden riches, the warriors invaded the region of Nineveh, Assyria's capital. Shortly afterwards, they signed a pact with the local rulers to fight Babylon and other rising civilizations.

FORTUNATE EXPANSION

The Scythians managed to rise socially by establishing colonies in the territories occupied today by Romania, Ukraine, Moldova, and some parts of Russia. Among the commercial actions adopted by the population, the most lucrative was to act as intermediaries between the Greeks and rural producers in other areas. Negotiations involved the export of honey, cereals, wheat, animal skins, wine, weapons, and very rare works of art. All the planning depended on the needs of each merchant, since in some places agricultural cultivation was hampered by the low fertility of the soil. Although economically successful, the Scythians were also expelled from the Caucasus by the Sarmatians. The Iranian population dominated the region with numerous and extremely violent troops. Archaeological materials found during research into the ruins of the site show several monuments covered in gold. During the first centuries of the Christian era, the Yuezhi people, spread throughout parts of Asia, declared war on the Scythians. It is not known exactly how this ancient civilization became extinct, but it is believed that successive violent conflicts were the main cause.

FAMILY RELATIONS

The civilization of the Thracians, considered by many theories to be direct relatives of the Cimmerians, was divided into large tribes in the territory of Thrace, in southwestern Europe. During the 5th century BC, they occupied extensions between northern Greece and southern Russia. According to accounts by Herodotus, the community was the second largest population in the world at the time. They worshipped various gods, including Orpheus, Princess Europa, and Dionysus. Their main deities later also became part of Greek mythology. They were known as great craftsmen in their work with ceramics, stone, animal bones and metal artifacts. They built countless bronze sculptures, painted vases with scenes from everyday life and produced gold mugs for the nobles.

> Stone stars found by researchers in Ukraine and the Caucasus region may have originated in the homeland of the Cimmerians. These archaeological artifacts have different characteristics from the stars related to the Scythian warriors later.

THE MAGICAL UNIVERSE OF SHANGRI-LA

16

BASED ON A WORLDWIDE BESTSELLER, THE STORY OF THIS TERRITORY IS INSPIRED BY THE FORMATION OF A TRUE SPIRITUAL PARADISE IN THE MIDST OF THE HIMALAYAN MOUNTAINS

In a totally mystical realm, the civilization of Shangri-La would be a point of spiritual balance in the world. The legendary story of a place where time does not pass as it does on Earth and all the inhabitants live harmoniously and happily was created by the English writer James Hilton in the literary work "Lost Horizon". Released in 1933, the book has become an important cultural reference preserved by many generations of adventurers. The narrative describes a magical territory supposedly hidden among the Himalayan mountains, on the plateau of Tibet. The tranquil atmosphere of the place is described as unattainable for humans living in ordinary cities. In order to experience this unique sense of serenity, it is necessary to find the mystical valley and adapt internally to the paradisiacal setting. Life in Shangri-La is so different from the world as we know it that its inhabitants do not age with the passage of time. All the characteristics of modern routine are forgotten in the mythology, transforming the feelings of the people, who absorb the energy emanating from the mysterious mountains.

REAL INSPIRATIONS

The inspiration for creating a mystical earthly refuge came from a region that became extremely popular after its great literary success. According to several theories, Hilton based it on the lands of Diqing, located in the Yunnan provinces of southwest China. The unprecedented commercial triumph of the book led to the name of the territory's capital being officially changed to Shangri-La, attracting thousands of tourists during 2001. Being completely hidden between mountains and lakes, it is believed that the area emanates a different energy to visitors who pass through. Inhabited by a population estimated to be almost 34% Tibetan, the valley follows all Asian cultural traditions and is internationally known for its rich soil used to produce medicinal herbs. Today, the zigzag-shaped mountains are a major attraction for groups of travellers looking for the monuments described in the book.

The geographical extension is centred on the Yunnan Environmental Preservation Area, called the Three Parallel Rivers by the locals. Archaeological records show that the community of 354,000 inhabitants was settled around 6,000 years ago by the Tubo aboriginal peoples. The legends spread by Hilton's narrative have also attracted several adventurers and treasure hunters to the area. Despite being a region linked to spirituality, mysticism and esotericism, the tourist part of Shangri-La has many restaurants, hotels, souvenir shops and tours organized by agencies. One of the most visited spots in the valley is the Ganden Sumtseling Monastery, China's best-known study monastery.

LOCAL CHARACTERISTICS

The territory of Shangri-La is 10,500 feet above sea level. The side effects of the altitude do not get in the way of visitors, as it is possible to visit all parts of the valley in just one day. The houses have a distinctive architecture, with influences typical of Tibetan culture, centred on the construction of large temples. Many local children help visitors by sharing historical information about the monuments linked to Hilton's literary myths. Some fans of Hilton's work believe that this great popularization and tourism in the region is totally contrary to the original concepts of paradise disseminated by the British writer. In the old centre of the community there are several ruins left by its settlers, displaying several houses designed in a simple, traditional style. From July to September, it rains almost daily in the valley, considerably deterring groups of visitors. In the other months of the year, the temperature can alternate between all the seasons on the same day. In the Tibetan language, the name Diqing means "auspicious region" because of the 26 different ethnic groups that live there. The existence of the community, nicknamed Shangri-La, only became known worldwide after the success of the book. The journey to the mystical paradise takes about four hours by bus on muddy roads.

MODERN EXHAUSTION

Many researchers believe that the great repercussion of the book at different times was due to the stressful climate caused by the conflicts of modern life. People must work hard; financial problems often take debtors' sleep away and family or emotional issues trigger anxiety and self-esteem crises on different scales. All these problems are causing a growing sense of exhaustion in humans. One of the messages conveyed in the book suggests directing people's gaze towards the really important issues, seeking a high level of spiritual quality in this world. The coexistence free of authoritarianism, accusations and questioning addressed by Hilton encourages the path of self-knowledge and spiritual freedom. In very particular ways, readers can adapt the book's characteristics of full happiness to their daily routine, believing that the existence of the mysterious paradise would be the ideal refuge to escape the chaos of today's society.

INTENSE REVERBERATION

As a result of the great success achieved by the myth of Shangri--La, the characteristics of the magical territory were incorporated into various artistic strands. Musical bands, public figures from various fields of production and Theosophical scholars contributed even more to spreading the stories about Hilton's narrative. Although the book reached a wide audience, many people only learned about the mystical elements present in the paradise region through the references used on other cultural platforms. Many recent literary publications also use the popularity of the local magician to boost public interest in their content. Written by Mitchell Zuckoff, the title "Lost in Shangri-La - A True Story of Survival and Adventure" tells the story of 24 American soldiers who board a cargo plane to take a brief aerial tour of the mystical area of ancient Diqing. Released in 2013, the narrative covers the accounts of three survivors who got to know the mountains and the local secrets in a different way. To date, two films have been produced from Hilton's work, released in 1937 and 1973.

LITERARY SYNOPSIS

The positivist message mixed with a great adventure turns the story of the famous book into inspiration for readers. Right from the start, James Hilton's text makes it impossible to know to what extent the events described in the book are true. The author tells us in detail about the Tibetan beliefs related to the existence of the magical territory and reveals how he was inspired by Diqing to compose all the mythological pieces of Shangri-La. The Himalayan valley was introduced to him by a friend during a meeting with former colleagues from the university he graduated from. In the text, four passengers take off from Baskul heading east, intending to fly over the Himalayan ranges, China, and Nepal. After several changes to the route, the aircraft is hijacked, but ends up crashing on one of the region's mountain peaks. The pilot is dead, while after a long wait, they are rescued by native monks who take them to Shangri-La. Disgruntled, the four characters are forced to stay in the mystical valley for 60 days, while they learn to connect with many secrets that will change their lives forever. Shortly after publication, the book won the Hawthornden Prize, an important award in British literature.

MAN VS. MYTH

The writer James Hilton (1900-1954) worked for a long time on movie scripts after releasing his best-selling novel. Recognized for his talent in the UK, he decided to leave for Hollywood in 1935 to work in various roles. He wrote his first novel, "Catherine Herself", at the age of 16, in 1920. Before the mythology of Shangri-La spread worldwide, he was a regular contributor to literary columns in various newspapers. Although he wrote other works in the meantime, his first successful experience came in 1934 with "Goodbye Mr. Chips". The novel, which dealt with an old professor in a simple way, aroused public interest in his previous texts, causing the meteoric rise of "Lost Horizon", released a year earlier. In addition to the mythological book, the narrative of "Heaven's Fury", from 1932, also fell to readers' liking. In the film industry, he adapted his own novels for the big screen, winning the Oscar for Best Adapted Screenplay for "Goodbye, Mr. Chips". He was also a talented radio narrator and became very popular in the United States for his various artistic endeavours. He wrote a multitude of books until his death in 1954 in California. Among his most important titles are "Love in a Time of Hate", released in 1933, "We Are Not Alone", from 1937, and "That Unforgettable Day", from 1945. In addition to adaptations of his own works, he made a name for himself in cinema with the narration of "Madame Curie", which premiered in 1943, and the screenplay for "The Lady of the Camellias", in 1956.

THE ISLAND OF MAGIC AND MYSTICISM

17

A SPECIAL PART OF ENGLISH MEDIEVAL LITERATURE, THE ENCHANTED ISLAND OF AVALON IS HOME TO THE STORIES OF KING ARTHUR AND OTHER SECRETS YET TO BE DISCOVERED

The island of Avalon became known worldwide as part of the legendary story of King Arthur. The place, which stands out for its mystical powers, is mentioned for the first time in the tale "Historia regum Britanniae", written by the Welshman Geoffrey of Monmouth in 1138. The magical elements of the territory identify it as the place where King Arthur's mighty sword, Excalibur, was forged. The island was said to have healing properties, welcoming the British character after a bloody conflict, to recover from serious injuries. Little is known about the region's origins, but its activities date back to the end of the 5th century, during the literary hero's battles against Saxon invasions of Britain. In some versions of local mythology, King Arthur is taken to a different version of Avalon that makes its inhabitants immortal, in a kind of parallel universe.

Over the centuries, the English have cultivated various legends surrounding the events related to the medieval character. According to mythology, the enchanted lands were commanded by the pagan priestess Viviane, the Lady of the Lake, who is also Arthur's aunt, accompanied by nine maidens charged with nursing the protagonist back to health on a bed of gold. Other theories, based on evidence found in the books, claim that the English hero could not resist the long journey after being wounded in a battle for command and ended up dying, throwing his sword into the lake of Avalon. His body was taken to be buried in a secret enchanted place on the island. The belief that inspired the development of British folklore defends yet another version of the monarch's supposed death. During the intense journey, he was only asleep, waiting for the right mo-

Excalibur: legendary sword used in the stories of King Arthur

ment to return to public life after being healed by the miraculous energy of the territory.

MAGICAL ARTS

The island is also said to be a powerful refuge for mystical spirits capable of altering the fate of mortals according to their sorcerous influences. In the historical tale "The Winter King", by British author Bernard Cornwell, Avalon is called Ynys Wydryn (Isle of Glass). The literary work is part of the famous trilogy about the saga of the mythological hero. The romantic fictional narratives mix legendary theories with historical facts from the history of England and the world. One of the most important figures on the site is the fairy Morgana, the literary monarch's half-sister. The young priestess is in the process of training to take Viviane's place as Lady of the Lake and lead the island. The folkloric wizard Merlin, who acted as one of the king's main advisors, also lived there. The important female figure in Asturian legend was the older sister of Igraine, King Arthur's mother, and was given the task of handing over the mystical sword to her nephew. In a ceremony held at spiritual points on the island, the protagonist of the story received Excalibur in front of Merlin and his half-sister Morgana. One of the promises made during the ritual guaranteed a government under the Kingdom of England following Catholic principles and the mystical dogmas of Avalon.

ANCIENT RELIGION

Avalon was, above all, a veritable school of ancient pagan gods. The knowledge shared in the territory spanned generations, with Merlin being the great lord of the region. The inhabitants studied the mystical past intensely, aided by priests of great political influence, who were divided into various functions. Merlin's powers were responsible for the construction of the mythological Tor Tower. There, the wizard kept all his treasures, including extremely powerful magical information. King Arthur's father, Uther Pendragon, who acted as sovereign of the Bretons, followed the principles of worship handed down by the Lady of the Lake for a long time. King Arthur's famous Round Table, cited in countless cultural productions, positioned all the knights of the troop in equal seats to symbolize the vision of an equal community before the sovereign and the local deities.

SACRED WATERS

As the local teachings were also part of his mother's beliefs, the hero of the literary saga undertook to propagate the pagan dogmas so that they would not be forgotten with the passage of time. According to English

Monument dedicated to the legends of King Arthur and Avalon in Cornwall, England

mythology, the character of Morgana despised all the fields of study practiced by this belief, becoming a problem in helping to save her brother. After being seriously wounded in battle, Morgana led Arthur to a boat to try to take him to Avalon. However, due to her questioning of the Lady of the Lake's powers, she was prevented from entering the magical island. To resolve the impasse, King Arthur had to return his sword to the waters, redeem his sister and thus reach the sacred lands. In different versions disseminated in British folklore, the figure of the priestess moved between the lake and the island's soil. A tomb for the heroic monarch would have been built in the region blessed by Merlin's mystical powers. Theories about the literary figure of the wizard went far beyond the works destined for the Arthurian cycle. The medieval character of Godfrey of Monmouth also appears in another series by the author, called "The Prophecy of Merlin", in which the text mixes popular legends from Wales. Over the centuries, writers of different nationalities have used the stories of the wizard and Arthur in their literary titles.

OFFICIALLY GLASTONBURY

A group of monks from Glastonbury Abbey, in the English county of Somerset, claimed to have found the bones of King Arthur and Queen Geneva buried in the territory. From 1190, the legendary Isle of Avalon officially became part of the Glastonbury region. The mystical area of the Arthurian stories is believed to be located within the county surrounded by marshes and filled with abundant apple trees, as described in the books. After the Saxons invaded English lands in the last years of the 5th century, this magical valley is said to have ceased to be Avalon and was renamed Glastonbury by the invaders. Located 31 miles south of Bristol, the town currently has an estimated population of 8,800. Involved in various religious, historical, and cultural theories, the county receives many tourists for Catholic pilgrimages and visits to the ruins of the Tor Tower, which in official records are just the remains of an ancient church. Despite housing the remaining monument of Glastonbury Abbey and having been extremely Catholic over the centuries, various movements linked to mystical beliefs and pagan ideologies still prevail in the area. From the city's high points, you can understand how the territory may have been geographically an island in the past, especially in winter when the fields are constantly flooded.

SACRED TEMPLE

Many scholars of British folklore claim that the theories that Glastonbury is the island of Avalon are false. For them, the discovery of King Arthur's tomb in the county shows that the site is just a path to the real Avalon. According to legends preserved by the Welsh, the island represents a kind of mysterious paradise full of love and beauty. The magical region would be the only way in the world to achieve immortality. The myth is related to the region's abundant and characteristic apple trees, which would refer to the Garden of Eden described in the Bible. The refuge is home to mythological beings, such as characters from the Arthurian saga, and knights with pure souls who have managed to find it. People from Ireland and other nearby regions also have a long list of legends about the popular mythology. The island functions very differently from other places in the world, making it impossible for suffering to reach its inhabitants. Adventurers, churchmen, and researchers have tried to find this refuge in various parts of Europe, such as Ireland, Wales, and the county of Cornwall.

MYSTERIOUS PORTAL

According to some aspects of English mythology, only those who believe in the existence of the mystical island will be able to find it. The mysteries of the land are intended only for those with purity of soul. The land of magic is also said to be inhabited by ancestral advisors destined to accompany the spiritual growth of their followers. Entry to this path of self-knowledge and universal learning would only take place through a magical portal, located beyond the waters of Glastonbury. The search for divine fulfilment in the place can be seen within each person who has faith in mythology, and the way to enter Avalon would lie within their own feelings. However, other legends claim that access to the territory

King Arthur's famous Round Table in Winchester, England

can only be gained through an enchanted cave on the side of a mountain. For the island's priests, this hill could be seen from long distances. For ordinary people, however, the portal was seen only as a large slope in the middle of calm waters. In one of the most popular versions of the myth, the group of local priests was led by Morgana, declared the new Lady of the Lake. One of her most protected secrets in Avalon would be the cup of healing used to save King Arthur. The place would emanate such peace that the conflicts between the heroic monarch and his half-sister reported in literary works would be completely forgotten.

Various legends about the existence of the Holy Grail, the sacred chalice that would represent the secret lineage of Jesus Christ and Mary Magdalene, were disseminated by English medieval romances. According to the mythological stories, after Christ's crucifixion, the Jew Joseph of Arimathea took the object to England, where he founded the country's first Christian congregation in Glastonbury. Over time, the Grail ended up being lost and falling into anonymity. The first person to search for the sacred artifact, which offers powers to those who possess it, is King Arthur. For him, the Grail is the only way to save his life and the existence of the kingdom of Camelot. The mythological character and his knights never found the religious object.

THE QUEST FOR AGARTTHA'S KINGDOM

18

THE MYSTICAL KINGDOM SUBMERGED INSIDE THE EARTH IS SHROUDED IN THEORIES PACKED WITH SCIENTIFIC STUDIES AND SPIRITUAL ARGUMENTS FROM BUDDHISM

The myth related to the kingdom of Agarttha has crossed the boundaries of time and has remained popular for over 140 years. Based on the complex theory of the Hollow Earth, the originally Buddhist legend represents one of the main topics of discussion between science and religion. The advanced underground civilization would be dominated by the mythological figure of the World King, composing an environment in which peace and spiritual balance predominate. The first account of the mystical kingdom's existence was given by French writer Louis Jacolliot in 1873. When detailing the characteristics of this people, he referred to the region as Agartha, which led to various speculations due to the similarity with the names the Norse gave to their gods. Another version of the legend states that the underground population lived in a modern system of caves and tunnels designed in isolated parts of the Himalayas, near India. Although it was discussed by several researchers at the time, the theory reached greater proportions when Polish writer, geologist and scientist Ferdynand Ossendowski published the book "Beast, Men and Gods". The work, which mixed scientific, religious, and political elements, talks about the mysterious land through the spiritual experience of elaborate characters. The place would be a kind of parallel world where the wind does not blow, the Earth does not move and the inhabitants breathe wisdom.

KING OF THE WORLD

The submerged city would be populated by thousands of inhabitants who live free of vices in a long process of searching for knowledge and inner peace. In the literary work, the King of the World, called Melchizedek, is portrayed as a highly respected divine figure, the most enlightened spirit among the universal spheres. According to mythological tradition, all existing life forms must revere the great spiritual king. Theories about the sovereign have been intensively studied and adopted as religious beliefs by many monks. The subject has also aroused the interest of researchers linked to the occult, such as the French writers René Guénon and Saint-Yves d'Alveydre. In order to enter the mystical lands of Agartha, theories state that it is necessary to have great inner faith in the existence of this place, full of tranquillity and good feelings. The kingdom would have direct contact with God through its sovereign, who is spiritually linked to all the divinities in the universe. Melchizedek would live in a great palace full of crystal-covered spaces, accompanied on his throne by groups of Spiritual Pandits and powerful deities with enough strength to destroy all of humanity if they feel challenged.

SHAMBALA MYTH

Although Ossendowski never made any comments on the subject, many researchers believe that he was inspired by the legendary stories of Shambala to compose his literary underground refuge. While working on the book, the writer visited places where the myth was created, such as Tibet and Mongolia. Typical of Tibetan Buddhism, the theory goes that Shambala is a mystical place located in a hidden spot in the Himalayas or near Siberia. Mentioned in various sacred texts over the centuries, the territory preserves the traditional teachings of the religion, providing a space of peace, balance, and happiness. According to the Tantra scriptures, one of the kings of Shambala received knowledge from Buddha about the highest form of Kalachakra Tantra practice.

The tradition of this philosophy tells us that when the world loses all existing good, the twenty-fifth king of the magical soil of the lands of Shambala will be revealed to fight the dark forces of evil. From then on, a new Golden Age will begin in various parts of the universe. Most versions of the legend in Tibet place the sacred region as the capital of the kingdom of Agarttha. The mysterious area could only be accessed through a secret portal. On passing through the entrance, a series of soft lights would lead the visitor to a large food plantation, grown in fertile soil to ensure a good quality of life for the inhabitants.

EXPANSION OF BELIEF

The sacred place would welcome its inhabitants according to their spiritual karma. It would be one of the necessary conditions for the candidate to enter the kingdom, to fully develop their capacity for inner evolution. Among the residents of the enlightened capital would be men of science, priests, missionaries, and Buddhist monks of advanced levels. The entire structure of the sacred territory would be very similar to the Potala Palace, the Dalai Lama's main residence in Lhasa, Tibet. Theories about the submerged civilization spread to various parts of the West in the mid-17th century. At the time, the Catholic missionaries Estêvão Cacella and João Cabral made trips to Tibet to try to uncover more information about the contents of the geographical extension of the place. The spiritual concepts surrounding life in Shambala were disseminated by groups of missionaries, explorers, scholars, occultists and, above all, by the principles of Theosophy defended by Helena Petrovna Blavatsky.

The Russian writer was largely responsible for introducing the myth into esoteric courses, arousing the interest of many adventurers in search of the mystical region. Many attempts to explain the geographical location of Shambala have been put forward by these groups, but none of them have been scientifically proven. According to the beliefs of Theosophy, all the inhabitants of the sacred territory belong to the ranks occupied by the wisest men in the world in the Great White Brotherhood. The first account of the area was by the Hungarian scholar Alexander Csoma de Körös.

POLITICAL INTEREST

With a narrative totally focused on anti-communism, Ferdynand Ossendowski allegedly used his legendary work to gain advantages in political relations. The Bolsheviks, the most radical members of the RSDLP (Russian Social Democratic Workers' Party), are identified in the text as antichrists that the holy kingdom was trying to combat. Knowing about Baron von Sternberg's extremist character against the situation of the communists in Russia, he tried to impress him by telling the stories covered in his work to further popularize the myth about the isolated civilization. Several hypotheses linked to the theosophical school claim that before Shambala was a submerged kingdom, there would have been an island in the territory, when central Asia was still covered by a large sea. The place would have been the first inhabited by the Lords of the Flame, known as the spiritual creators of human beings, after arriving from Venus. Currently, what remains of the White Island, as it is folklorically known, would be protected from invasion by spiritual beings in the Gobi Desert, between China and the southern region of Mongolia. Groups of occultists integrated into Nazism in Germany saw mystical legends as a strong source of power capable of dominating the spiritual energies of the universe. They took advantage of funding for studies supported by the German government to investigate more information about the myth, developing some texts centred on the subject.

HOLLOW EARTH

Over the centuries, some representatives of the scientific community have carried out research to confirm the Hollow Earth theory. According to their claims, the planet is a hollow body with several cracks located at the geographic poles. The inner areas would be inhabited by technologically advanced peoples. These mysterious beings would get to know parts of the Earth through visits carried out in UFOs. The renowned British astronomer and mathematician Edmund Halley, responsible for discovering Halley's Comet, was one of the first academics to defend the existence of this submerged territory. Devoted to religion and God-fearing, Halley believed that the city inside the Earth must be populated by spiritual beings.

Based on years of studies into the inconstancies of the Earth's magnetic field, he developed the theory of the Four Spheres, a phenomenon that could be the cause of the Aurora Borealis, which occurs in polar regions. Nowadays, science has come up with other accurate explanations of the movements of the electromagnetic sphere inside the Earth, but Halley's research has never been completely discredited.

SPIRITUAL NATURE

Tibetan theories about Shambala believe that the appearance of the magical underground territory varied according to the spiritual nature of each person who observed it. It would function as a kind of mirror reflecting their feelings and forming an environment corresponding to the needs of individual religious studies. One of the main concepts of these Buddhist practices is to develop such an advanced level of knowledge that it allows the monk to intuitively find the spiritual path to the blessed lands. Speculation has it that the American government sent an expedition to Antarctica based on the information disseminated in the books to try to find the secret portal. Although they did not get any concrete results, the researchers discovered that that part of the planet formed a continent. The secret society Vril, formed by powerful names from German Nazism, is also said to have financed several attempts to locate Shambala. Extremely interested in extraterrestrials, they believed in the possibility of finding the UFOs mentioned by science. The main objective of Hitler's men was to discover, through subterranean beings, how to manipulate spaceships in order to use them in wars. According to their research, Eskimos and animals would also live inside the Earth after death.

LESS KNOWN, BUT VERY IMPORTANT

19

ALTHOUGH THEY HAVE NOT BEEN REPORTED
SO PROMINENTLY BY RESEARCH TEAMS,
THESE CIVILIZATIONS HAVE ALSO AROUSED
INTEREST IN THEIR CULTURE OVER
THE CENTURIES

Ruins of the city of Mohenjo-daro

Although they expressly contributed to important discoveries in archaeology, some lost cities ended up receiving less attention in historical and academic contexts. The Harappan culture, for example, was forgotten for several centuries until excavations in 1920 revealed traces of its existence. The people of the Indus Valley civilization rose during the Bronze Age, between 4000 BC and 1300 BC, being one of the first three societies formed in the Old World alongside Mesopotamia and ancient Egypt. Its territorial domains were in northwestern South Asia, extending to parts of Afghanistan, Pakistan, and India. During their heyday, the population may have reached more than 5 million people, forming a series of communities scattered throughout the valley, sharing the same customs.

The architectural productions built in the Indus show advanced urban distribution techniques and efficient drainage systems. Large complexes of buildings and residential houses were erected and equipped with water supply schemes. Among the commercial activities developed were the production of handicrafts, specializing in seal sculptures and metallurgical work with copper, lead, and bronze. Jewellery, stamps, and garments were also traded. Research at the site found the first ruins of the city of Harappa on land now belonging to Pakistan. It is believed that the territory was a kind of commercial centre for the valley, concentrating all the administrative power of the society. Excavation work around the archaeological site subsequently revealed important regions such as Mohenjo-daro, one of the largest population provinces of the ancient civilization. According to researchers, there is no evidence of violence among the ruins found. It seems that the cities were impoverished by changes related to the arid climate of the territory. The agricultural system would have collapsed after the disappearance of the Saraswati River, alternating a long period between droughts and floods, and resulting in the disappearance of the Harappan civilization.

REFINED CONSTRUCTIONS

The Neolithic settlement of Çatalhöyük reached a refined architectural stage around 6700 B.C. Existing in the Anatolian regions, they built a series of spacious houses entered through the roof. As the site had no space for streets, it is believed that the passage between the dwellings took place through strategic connections adapted at the top. The archaeological site with the ruins of the ancient society is now a UNESCO World Heritage Site. Before constructing the houses, the population drew up a kind of blueprint showing the necessary divisions in the space. The houses had specific horizontal platforms for sleeping. Other rooms showed concern for the areas dedicated to work. In addition to these divisions, homes also had stoves in rooms used exclusively for preparing food.

Ceramic pieces decorated the interior of the buildings, accompanied by murals showing repeated drawings. Among the sculptures found by archaeologists, numerous female figures caught the attention of researchers. It is believed that the works were intended to symbolize the fertility of the region's women. Most of the artistic activities were made from bones placed in a system of molds. Around 18 different levels of technique were found in the artifacts, made with delicate and precise strokes. The residential environments were divided into clean and dirty places. Scholars believe that the unhygienic parts functioned as a garbage dump. After the death of members of the civilization, the bodies were buried inside the houses in a fetal position. To date, the causes that led to the extinction of Çatalhöyük remain a mystery.

CAHOKIA CITY

Currently, the ruins left by this indigenous civilization have become the Cahokia Mounds State Historic Site. The territory lies between a plain east of Saint Louis and Collinsville, in southwestern Illinois, USA. In its period of activity, between the 600s and 1400s, the region had a geographical extent larger than London. Its settlements began to be built more than five centuries before the arrival of Europeans on the American continent. Around 80 mounds made of earth and wood by the Indians have been preserved at the site, which is open to visitors. The distribution of the small isolated hills was carried out in the form of a complex solar calendar, marking the seasons. Studies into the pre-urbanization work at Cahokia are still ongoing.

ANCIENT CULTS

The sanctuary of Göbekli Tepe is the oldest place of worship in the world found by archaeologists. It is located on top of a hill in the Tauro Mountain range in southwestern Turkey. Built around the third millennium by hunter-gatherers, the structure is 49.2 feet high and 180 in diameter. It is speculated, given the state of the sanctuary's ramifications, that it may have been used as early as the Mesolithic period. Inside, the temple features illustrations of bulls, lions, birds, arachnids, and reptiles. According to researchers, there is no possibility that the figures represented a written language. The discoveries made by German teams have revolutionized what was previously known about theories related to local religiosity. Many legends speculate that the region is an extension of the Garden of Eden, mentioned in the Bible as the place built by God to house Adam and Eve.

Throughout the research process, other settlements were found in the area. Megalithic monuments, such as houses or temples, displayed figures similar to those of the sanctuary stamped on the walls. The ones that come closest to representing human forms are located on the pillars of some buildings. Vultures are the animals most often depicted on buildings. It is believed that the dead of the civilization were left exposed on the ground for the vultures to devour. American researchers visited Göbekli Tepe for excavations in 1964. In their findings, they assessed that the hill region could not have been built without the participation of human communities. However, they only officially registered the area as an abandoned Byzantine cemetery. The work of the German Archaeological Institute began in 1994, supported by the Museum of Şanlıurfa. As the prehistoric population was in the habit of removing rocks to clear the land, much of the researched material has deteriorated, making new discoveries difficult.

NABTA PLAYA

The region is known for its many archaeological sites. Located in the Nubian Desert, the area was extremely fertile around 1000 BC. A large sequence of rains made it possible for a lake to form, improving living conditions in the area. The first people to inhabit the area were

Archaeological site in Anatolia, Turkey

attracted by the favourable climate and the possibility of raising cattle in the pastures. According to archaeological records, the ascendant societies in Nabta Playa were the first to domesticate large herds in Africa. The territory reached northeast Sudan between the River Nile and the Red Sea. The population developed ceramic techniques full of complex inscriptions on the pieces. During the seventh millennium BC, there was a large settlement in the region that used deep water wells built to guarantee an annual supply. Agricultural production at the time revolved around vegetables, corn, fruit, sorghum, and tubers.

According to scholars, goats and sheep coming from the northeast of the territory contributed to the commercial advance of the place. Their villages were built with planned arrangements of stones above and inside the ground. Some researchers claim that the desert had such mild characteristics only in summer, causing the population to migrate to other locations for the rest of the year. One of the main constructions at Nabta Playa is one of the oldest archaeoastronomical devices discovered in the history of archaeology. The large monument, made up of huge rocks, indicated the appearance of the stars at different times and the location of the Sun. The site is still being studied with references included in official UNESCO documents.

KHMER EMPIRE

The Angkor region served as the base for the powerful Khmer empire. Located in Cambodia, the civilization existed roughly between the 9th and 13th centuries. In 2007, an intensive international research project concluded, based on satellite images, that the territory would have functioned as the largest pre-industrial city in the world. An advanced urbanization project linked the area of 390 square miles among all the nuclei formed by the local temples. Little is known about the social structure of the Khmer Empire; however, geological evidence has proven the advance of large agricultural fields in a society large enough to feed millions of inhabitants. With extremely modern architectural methods, the population was responsible for building a series of luxurious temples. More than a thousand monuments have been found among the ruins of the archaeological site. Among them is Angkor Wat, considered the largest religious construction in the world. Today, all the areas belonging to the civilization of the past are on the UNESCO World Heritage List. Most of the ruins have been restored and have become an important historical centre open to tourists, receiving more than 2 million visitors a year. Angkor's territorial dominance lasted until 1431, when Thai peoples invaded the region, causing the community to migrate to Phnom Penh.

RELIGIOUS SCRIPTURES

Mythologically, the city of Ubar became known as a Muslim version of the lost continent of Atlantis. Mentioned by the Koran as a civilization existing in the southern region of the Arabian desert, the territory was nicknamed the Atlantis of the Sands. During the history described by Islam's holy book, the population, called the Ad, is said to have built countless buildings and developed an important administrative hierarchy. Impressed by the rise of the region, the inhabitants ended up deviating from Allah's teachings. Concerned about the direction of the city, the Arab deity sent the prophet Hub. In completely arrogant acts, the Ad people claimed that they no longer needed teachings. Allah, furious, decided to punish them with a sandstorm lasting eight days and seven nights. Faced with the damage caused to the territory, all the inhabitants disappeared. In 1990, using images captured by NASA satellites, American archaeologists found traces left by the city of Ubar. The evidence consisted of camel routes and administrative occupations. Despite the presentation of the material, the site's connection with the myth of Atlantis of the Sands has not yet been scientifically confirmed.